Log Home Inspirations

4880 Lower Valley Road, Atglen, PA 19310

Roger Wade &
Tina Skinner

Acknowledgments

The beautiful homes in this book are found all over the United States, from the desert mountains of Arizona to the Northern Woods of Wisconsin, and from the eastern farmlands of Pennsylvania to a southern lake in the Carolinas. Though they vary in design and style, each has one thing in common, they were all designed, manufactured, and constructed in coordination with Expedition Log Homes of Wisconsin. To learn more about Expedition and their complete custom home planning services, visit their website at www.expeditionloghomes.com or call 877-250-3300.

Design featured on Page 60 by:
LAN Associates
252 Main Street
Goshen, NY 10924
845-615-0350
www.lan-nj.com

Designs featured on Pages 101 and 116 by:
Distinctive Homes
PO Box 3988
Prescott, AZ 86302
928-771-0948
www.distinctivehomesaz.com

All Other Designs by:
Expedition Log Homes, LLC
PO Box 700080
Oostburg, WI 53070
877-250-3300
www.expeditionloghomes.com

Photograph of Expedition Owners, Page 4 by:
Dennis Schwartz Photography
307 E. Mill Street
Plymouth, WI 53073
920-893-8989

Library of Congress Control Number: 2006940465

Designed by "Sue"
Type set in American Typewriter Md BT/Zurich BT

ISBN: 978-0-7643-2655-4
Printed in China

Published by Schiffer Publishing Ltd.
4880 Lower Valley Road
Atglen, PA 19310
Phone: (610) 593-1777; Fax: (610) 593-2002
E-mail: Info@schifferbooks.com

For the largest selection of fine reference books on this and related subjects, please visit our web site at **www.schifferbooks.com**
We are always looking for people to write books on new and related subjects. If you have an idea for a book please contact us at the above address.

This book may be purchased from the publisher.
Include $3.95 for shipping.
Please try your bookstore first.
You may write for a free catalog.

In Europe, Schiffer books are distributed by
Bushwood Books
6 Marksbury Ave.
Kew Gardens
Surrey TW9 4JF England
Phone: 44 (0) 20 8392-8585; Fax: 44 (0) 20 8392-9876
E-mail: info@bushwoodbooks.co.uk
Website: www.bushwoodbooks.co.uk
Free postage in the U.K., Europe; air mail at cost.

Contents

Foreword

Cross the threshold of a log home for the first time and you are transported into a different world. Instantly at ease, you are embraced by the warmth and beauty of your environment. Wood has that quality about it. Its natural beauty and rusticity nourishes and renews the soul. Spend some time with log homeowners and you realize that each is as unique and full of character as the logs used to create their places of refuge.

Expedition Log Homes was created through a shared passion for the natural character and beauty of wood found in log homes, and has grown through a commitment to providing quality products and services. This shared vision has led to a business environment founded upon honest, straightforward dealings with others.

We pride ourselves in using a process that starts with raw logs harvested from sustainable forests. We control waste by cutting to yield (creating the best piece from each log) and make total use of each tree through the additional manufacture of farm bedding and landscape mulch. We provide superior quality by kiln-drying and enhance the natural beauty by hand-crafting with a drawknife. High energy-efficiency is obtained using the half-log construction methods featured in these pages.

Design is the canvas upon which our logs are displayed and each project has the opportunity to set new standards. The design ideas presented within these pages all began with a personal vision from individual homeowners. We work closely with all of our customers and collaborate to bring that vision to life. Creativity and craftsmanship go hand in hand. That's why each Expedition home is custom designed and tailor-made to your specifications.

It is an honor and a privilege to share this log home experience with our customers, field representatives, employees, and families. We can honestly say that the most rewarding part of this business is the lifetime friendships that we've made along the way.

We thank our customers whose homes and stories are featured within these pages for opening up their homes to inspire you.

If you'd like more information on our products and services call us at 877-250-3300. Or visit us online at www.expeditionloghomes.com.

McCabe Garcia Jan Koepsell Greg Grimes
Co-Owners
Expedition Log Homes, LLC

Introduction

In almost every conversation with a log home dweller, the word "cozy" comes out. Invariably, this same person's log home includes a "great room" with a cathedral ceiling that soars an extra story above the ground floor, outlined in great log beams and rafters. Within this soaring space there's usually enough room for a huge stone fireplace, a modern kitchen, a dining area, and a sitting area that takes advantage of a fabulous view framed by a wall of glass. Still, with all this air and magnificence around them, homeowners say they feel, well, right at home.

The warmth of natural logs keeps it all in scale, and the traditional simplicity of exposed beams and posts appeals to people on a deeply emotional level. As many homeowners relate, their log homes help them capture the same laid-back feeling they get after two weeks camping in a mountain log cabin; a feeling of vacation every day. Somehow, the return to ancestral architecture helps usher in an earlier time when life was less hectic. At least, once the door is closed.

This book ushers you through the front door and gives you a firsthand tour of seventeen fabulous houses and a log-built restaurant, inside and out. The homeowners share their experiences designing and building their dream homes. Their ideas will inspire you to design and build your own perfect every-day retreat. And their stories will reassure you that this home will be the one you'll want to come home to every day forever.

One Inspired Story

Two homeowners, Lana and Charles Sangmeister, were so enthusiastic about their home that they sent in a written essay a few days after they were interviewed. Their home and story are featured as Mountain Majesty later in the book, but their thoughts are shared here:

What we love most about our log home?

We love the fact that we had so much design flexibility with how we finished our home, yet were able to create a totally uncompromising exterior full-log look. From our research, this was only possible with a product line like Expedition Log Homes offered. We were able to pick an exterior look that is very much at home in the mountains of Montana, yet have everything else we wanted too, like a combination of log, tongue and grove, and sheetrock for the interior. We also were able to run our plumbing and electrical lines in the 2x6" insulated walls, which helped to lower our labor costs. This was possible because Expedition's expertise is with half-logs. Yet we have the full-log corner look on the outside that we loved so much and on the inside of our home, we were able to do everything that we wanted, even use our existing traditional furniture. It just turned out beautifully for us! It was so much fun to design and then to decorate.

What was the design process like?

Initially we thought we'd find an existing plan that we liked and would work with Expedition just to customize it. But we spent a lot time looking and never felt like we saw a plan that really addressed everything that we wanted. When that happened, we sketched out on a piece of paper the basic layout that we were thinking about and started an interactive process with Expedition's team that resulted in a one-of-a-kind home for us. There were hundreds of decisions to make, but they knew exactly the questions to ask. They made it all seem so easy! While we were focusing on our evolving floor plan, Expedition designers were busy making sure that our home was engineered correctly. The most challenging part for us was trying to envision what we were creating as we went along. Whenever we were struggling, Expedition would send us photos via email, which demonstrated what they were trying to explain to us. We even remember one time when our local representative took us to an Expedition home that had "double cathedral" ceilings – it really helped to see "double cathedrals" in person. We enjoyed the whole process. Before we knew it, we had signed-off on our plans!

What is it like living in a log home?

We are constantly pinching ourselves, we feel so lucky. Our home is so beautiful to us. We have a lot of interior wood touches – some half-log walls, tongue and groove wall and ceilings, rustic log beams and rafters, and even an open log staircase, which has resulted in a very warm, rich, and cozy interior feel. Our home also has a very secure feeling to it – a real sense of permanence. Because it is a frame-home with log siding, it is also very energy efficient. This was important to us because of Montana's four-season climate. One of the things that we like most, though, is how well it fits in the mountains of Montana. We always dreamed of having a log home in the Beartooth Mountains and now we have it!

Any advice you have for folks wanting a log home?

Our experience has been so positive. We think that is due to the fact that we did our research and we chose a great company to provide our log home package – all providers are not equal! We also had a builder that we were able to work well with – that is very important too.

We'd also suggest that if someone is dreaming about a log home, go for it now, don't wait until after retirement or some other milestone has been reached. Log homes really can set the stage for folks to live the life that they've been dreaming about.

Big, Happy Family

Seven family members pose in front of their fireplace, the hearth of a growing home!

A big family and a desire to keep it simple dictated the design of Mark and Teresa Bettag's home. Their children would share dorm-like rooms and one bath, and the family areas needed to be spacious and easy to keep clean.

"When we moved to this town we had two kids," Mark recalls of their introduction to Wisconsin. "By the time we moved we had five kids. We looked at adding on to our house so we could stay in our neighborhood, but we would have had no yard."

When it seemed they might burst at the seams, they consulted the man who'd built their first house, and together they started planning a log home on a ten-acre spread nearby. The plan involved two large dormitory rooms for the children upstairs, along with a master suite. Downstairs they wanted a spacious, open area where the family could congregate.

The plan was a little challenging, says Jan Koepsell of Expedition Log Homes. "Though it looks simple enough, it had a complicated roofline. With three major rooflines converging into one space, it was demanding from an engineering standpoint."

And worth the effort!

"What I like is that the house isn't cut up," said Mark Bettag, "so there's a big room where the kitchen, dining area, and family room are all intertwined. That's nice because we can see everybody and what everybody is doing." His favorite place is a workshop below the garage. "In the old house I had a workshop below the children's room and when they went to bed I had to stop work. The kids like going in the workshop to help me, too, so that's nice."

"I love the visibility," Teresa Bettag said. "We built it with family and function in mind. Even though it's much bigger than our previous home and apartments that we had, it's easier to clean and take care of. It's bright, with the clear finish on the logs. It just makes the house that much more bright. I am one of those types of people that needs order. With nine of us living in the house, it has some sense of order. We're very informal people, we don't have a formal dining room or living room, so it's a great place for everyone to gather. It's a very warm and inviting house. We really enjoy it. I'm blessed beyond belief to come home to this everyday."

The logs in the great room help to absorb sound. "It's very, very quiet," Teresa said. "We have a basement, so kids can be down there playing ping pong or upstairs in the loft studying. It's actually very quiet. Many people have said that, when they bring their kids over you'd never know there were more than ten kids there," With so many family members under one great roof, "there's never a dull moment," she concluded.

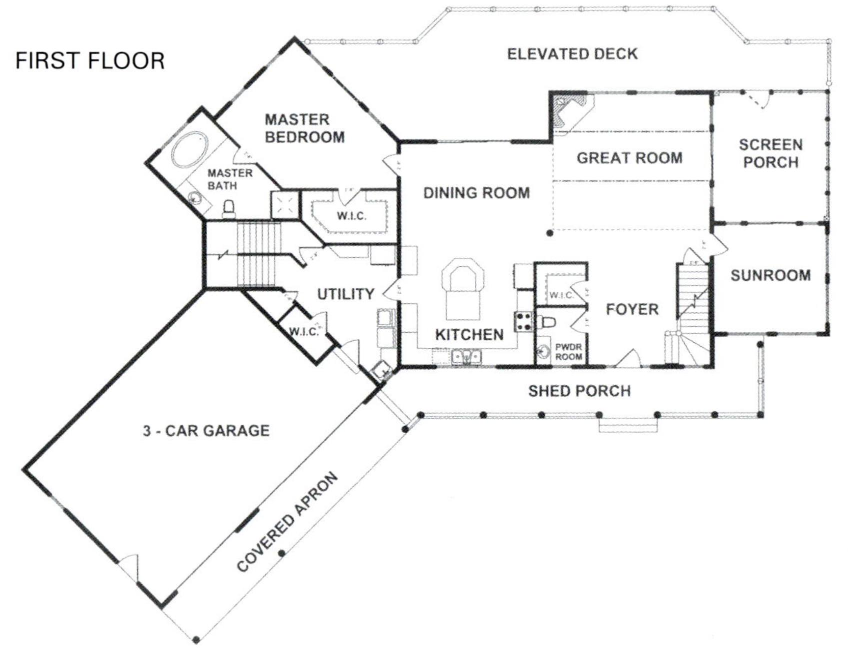
FIRST FLOOR
ELEVATED DECK
MASTER BEDROOM
MASTER BATH
W.I.C.
DINING ROOM
GREAT ROOM
SCREEN PORCH
SUNROOM
UTILITY
W.I.C.
KITCHEN
W.I.C.
PWDR ROOM
FOYER
SHED PORCH
3 - CAR GARAGE
COVERED APRON

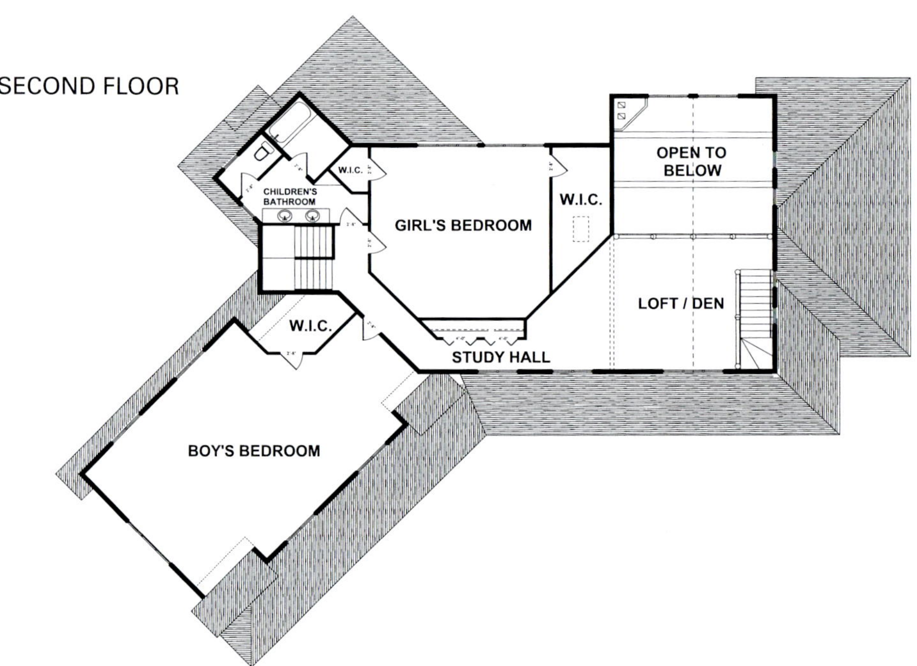
SECOND FLOOR
W.I.C.
CHILDREN'S BATHROOM
GIRL'S BEDROOM
W.I.C.
OPEN TO BELOW
LOFT / DEN
W.I.C.
STUDY HALL
BOY'S BEDROOM

Set on ten acres of fun, this family of nine enjoys plenty of play space, both inside and out.

The great room is the one place where the log system was brought inside, with 12-inch milled half rounds mounted on a stud wall. The owners wanted to keep many of their rooms white, but log molding was incorporated for window and door surrounds.

In the Bettag household, the dining area gets used daily. The space is defined by a large piece of linoleum that Teresa stenciled on a piece of durable linoleum and besides eliciting lots of compliments, it has proven a perfect, low-maintenance surface for a high-traffic family.

Teresa Bettag designed the kitchen, with maple cabinetry, a cherry theme, and granite countertops.

A hand-painted table and chairs are eye-catchers in a bright sunroom that opens to a screened-in porch.

"The bench by the windows was given to us by our builder, John Zelm," Mark said. "He gave that to us as a housewarming gift when we moved in. He built our first house in Sheboygan, and we knew he would be our builder when we moved again. They were very innovative, the builders, with lots of suggestions. They suggested we put a pantry in, and we're so glad we did."

A modest master bedroom on the first floor.

Frontal View

The Callahan family is shown shortly after moving into their new log home. Young Emma is now bigger, with a little sister to play with.

In love with the log look, Barbara and Matthew Callahan incorporated it into three structures on their Pennsylvania property: a house, a shed, and a doghouse for their pet beagles.

"We had always wanted to build a log home," Barbara said. To gather ideas, she subscribed to a log home magazine for half a dozen years, filing away pictures that appealed to them. Then they toured as many model homes as they could find, though "there aren't too many in our area."

The Callahans lived in a mobile home on their property for some time before construction began. They knew what would work with their lot, a front faced mostly in windows. Therefore their great room is just off the foyer, and a deck that runs the length of the home doubles as front porch.

"We knew we definitely wanted a great room. We wanted the great room, kitchen, and dining room all to be near each other, to make it easy to entertain and socialize."

The new home was constructed just behind their mobile home, which was removed soon after they moved in. Their baby daughter, Emma, was born just after they took up residence, and another daughter has since joined the family.

"For us it was somewhat of a smooth process because we had planned for so long," Barbara said. "There weren't a lot of last-minute decisions because we knew what we wanted to build for so long."

The result was a house they wouldn't change. "I love the coziness of it," Barbara said of her home. "My favorite room is the loft, which overlooks the great room. We have a computer up there, and sometimes I do work, or email friends and family. It's cozy up there, there's a couch. It's real pretty if you're up there and it's snowing because you can see out the windows. It's very serene; very peaceful."

FIRST FLOOR

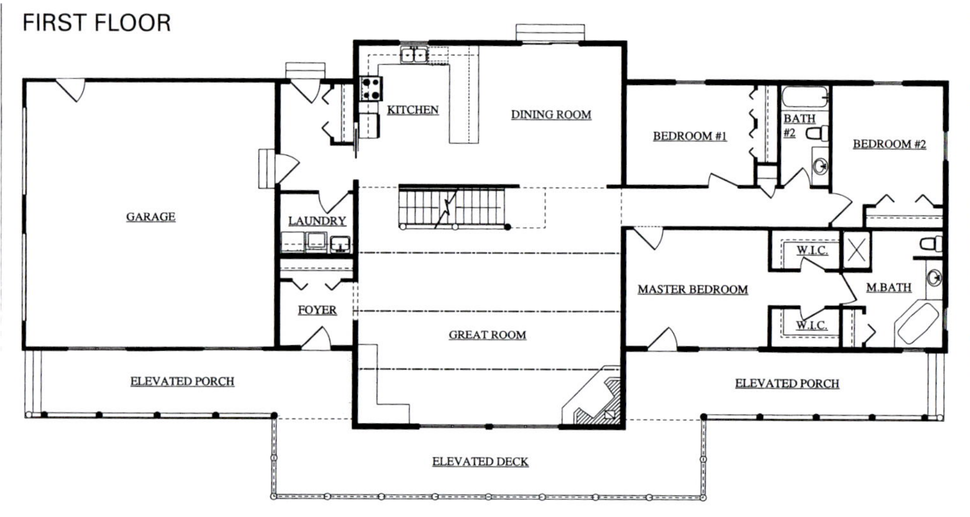

SECOND FLOOR

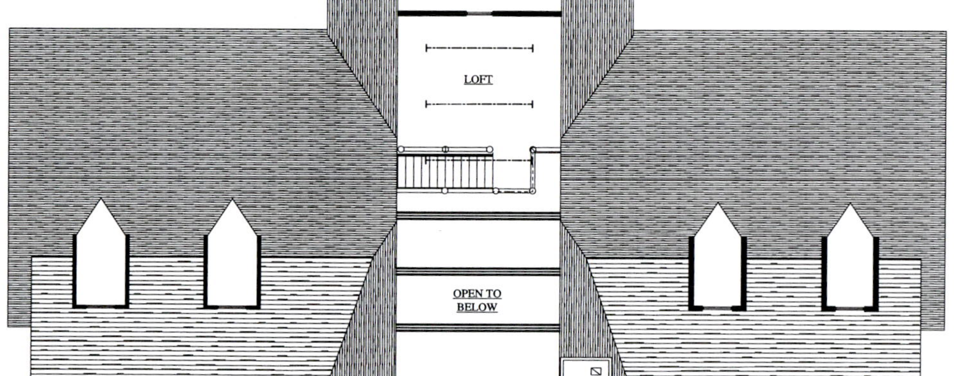

Because of the privacy offered by their lot, the homeowners created their deck and porch areas, as well as focusing most of their windows, out the front. Gabled dormers on the outside create character and add lighting to the interior. The entire exterior was faced in half logs.

A small log stand provides a greeting in the Callahan's foyer.

In addition to the home, the Callahans built a workshop/shed faced in logs, and Matthew Callahan even clad a dog kennel for their beagles in half-logs to match the home.

The fireplace and entertainment center act as counterweights in the great room, bookends to a trapezoid-shaped, fixed-frame window. Awning windows along the bottom of the great room's wall of glass provide ventilation without obstructing the view. Beside the fireplace, a small door opens to a wood box on the deck outside, eliminating the need to haul wood through the house. Note how canned lights were set in the paneled ceiling to illuminate the interior, above structural tie beams that emphasize the width of the great room.

Besides pocket lights in the ceiling, two art-glass globes hang over the kitchen's peninsula counter.

A shot of the dining room details how the doorways were framed with log.

This ranch style home included a loft area upstairs for a home office. The loft features half-log siding for trim around the circle-top window. It's a beautiful look possible only in a half-log home.

Two little girls enjoy private rooms in the Callahan home.

A wing of the home was dedicated to bedrooms, half for the master suite, the other half for children's rooms. In the master bath, the tub was faced with half logs, creating a charming tie-in with the rest of the home.

22 Arizona Escape

A retirement home in Arizona is pure mountain lodge, inside and out, with lots of log for the interior and exterior, as well as stone finishes and wildlife adornments. The use of wood and animal trophies announces the family's love of hunting and the outdoors, and picture windows left unobstructed reflect their desire to stay connected with Nature.

To fully enjoy the outdoors, decks, porches, and balconies are readily accessible from the kitchen, the master bedroom, the living room, and the entry. The home fits beautifully into its wooded lot in a private golf course community. Its appearance, and its layout, was designed to fit the land, leaving as many mature trees standing around the home as possible.

Swedish cope sidings with Swedish cope saddle notch interlocking log corners were used to give this home its beautiful façade. "Because it is an insulated log home, we were able to do the log picture frames around the windows on the exterior," said Jan Koepsell of Expedition Log Homes. "That's only possible because it is a half-log home."

Opposiite page:
A rear elevation image shows how the house seems to spread out along its wooded incline, and how a host of trees was preserved to help shield the home from the Arizona sun.

This page:
Because the outdoors is so important to these homeowners, the porch was decorated like a living room. Comfortable chairs cozy up to a stone fireplace. It also includes a big gas barbecue and mounted television set, with a view overlooking the golf course. This is Arizona, so there're no problems with bugs on the porch and/or moisture issues with appliances.

The great room has tile floor throughout, including the kitchen and out onto the porch.

A three-way fireplace in the dining and kitchen room was created with native stone found throughout the nearby forest. The character log mantelpiece is topped by a mountain lion.

Drywall was used in the kitchen to allow the cabinets an environment of their own, and a garden window was set in the wall above the sink. Stainless steel appliances emphasize the modern utility of this space.

A loft off of master bedroom area was furnished with a wonderful half-log end table, and the lounge chair provides an enticing reading nook.

The homeowners are obviously morning people. Like the other rooms in their home, this one leaves the windows open to the early sunlight. A three-sided fireplace faces both master bedroom and the loft. In the master bath, a favorite stained-glass window made by a family member was brought from the previous house, and a special place reserved for it in the new one.

Built for the Memories

You would think they were going to sell it, the way Dave and Hanne Duke go on and on about the location of their second home in the woods of Wisconsin. However, this home was built with an eye toward a long family tradition.

"When my father retired, he built a cabin in the mountains in Utah," Dave said. "We would come out from New York and go to that cabin in the mountains. There are a lot of memories of our family at 'Grandpa's cabin'. After he died, we kept that cabin for many years, but eventually we sold it. We thought it would be nice to start doing the same thing with our children and their families. We want to have our family memories that go on for generations."

The Duke cabin was actually built as part of a family enterprise, the investment being a joint effort of the Dukes and their four grown children. Daughter, Debbie, and her husband, Gregg, were directly involved in supervising the design and construction, while the rest of the family were happy to make suggestions and hear about the progress.

They modified an existing log home plan offered by Expedition Log Homes, adding a screened porch where they take most of their meals, and making other adjustments to maximize space. They are very happy with their new second home and they can't say enough about the location!

"It's right on a small, private lake with very few homes," explains Hanne. "It's a 'quiet' lake, which means no loud motors or boats. Deer, fox, and other wildlife walk through the property. It's like *On Golden Pond* – very peaceful. You can even hear the loons calling."

Besides peace and privacy, there's fishing to be enjoyed, Dave adds. And they've got lots of view. "Facing the lake we have about three stories of windows, the basement, first, and second floors," he said.

"We wanted a place that would be very good for our children and our grandchildren to be able to be together," Dave says. "We wanted them to be able to be close to nature and away from the noise, hustle, and bustle of the cities where they live."

Hanne added "It is a warm, cozy, and inviting home. Nobody wants to leave when they are here."

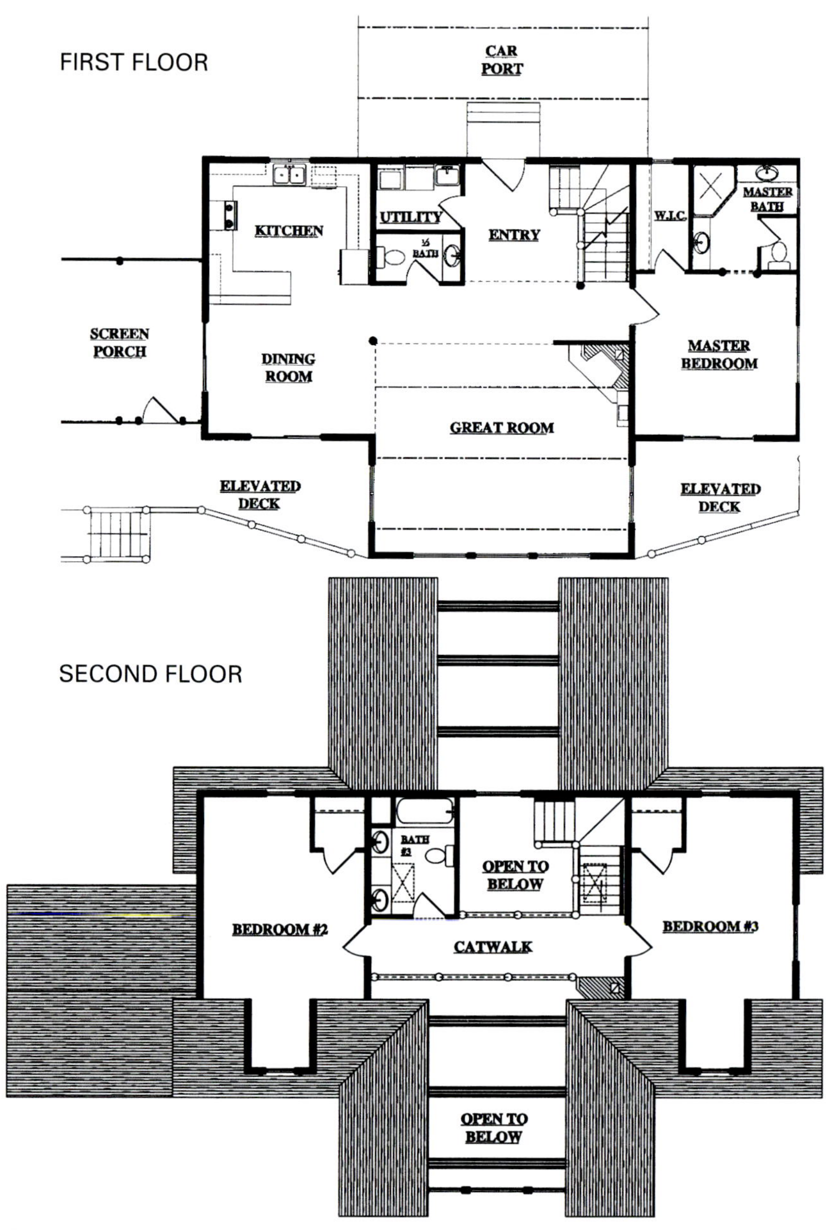

A canopy of beautiful fall leaves welcomes the Duke family to their new getaway in Northern Wisconsin. The front entry features a covered, step-gable drive-up. The overhead gable porch features a log tie beam with king post and diagonals to create a log truss. The corner near the screened porch shows the full round butt & pass corner that showcases the handcrafted beauty of Expedition's notching system. The house gains a sense of rustic design from the variable height half logs used in its siding.

Looking from the back, this vacation getaway features a walk-out basement and elevated decks to capitalize on the lakefront view. All of the windows and doors were trimmed with half-round logs. Symmetrical dormers balance the view of the home from the lake. Stone was used to face the center portion of the exposed basement, and cedar shake on either side.

The great room is illuminated by fixed picture windows that rise in a trapezoid. Windows on the sidewalls open to cross-ventilate the room. However, with the mosquitoes that thrive in the neighborhood, the family likes to air condition the interior of their home, and use a screened porch or decks when they want to sit "outside." The fireplace hearth was curved to allow it to protrude into the room and is covered with the same stone that is used on the outside of the home. A "character log" makes a fitting mantel.
The log stairway to the loft area incorporates inset metalwork, as does the balcony banister and the stairway down to the lower level.

The kitchen takes on its own identity with green-stained cabinetry. A structural log character post supports the floor above. Stone was used to face the kitchen peninsula, where the grandchildren like to sit. A farmhouse sink completes the rustic feeling.

The catwalk between the upstairs bedrooms overlooks the great room. Above, is a bird's-eye view of the double cathedral ceiling, where the great room ties into the center gable of the main house.

A screened porch, complete with a ceiling fan, has become the favorite hangout for the family. Hanne says, "we eat most of our meals here and it's a great place to play games."

The master bedroom was finished in knotty pine paneling and furnished with a log bed. The attached master bath has separate vanities, a shower, and heated floor.

The grandchildren bunk upstairs where lots of room has been set up for them. Each bunk features a full-size bed on the bottom and a twin on top. There are window seats and built-in drawers.

Solid Wood

After five years of living in his log home, Conrad Golanka is still gushing. "What we love most is the uniqueness of it, and the ability to, when you build them, to really, really put your personality into it. I think they are more adaptable than conventional building. You can make them to really fit your personality."

Perhaps the home has even altered his personality? "You don't build these homes and not have a sense of pride and want to share it with people," he said. "It gives you a sense of pride. People driving by will do a double take, and even stop. It makes you an exhibitionist a little bit." He said that local builders sometimes call and ask if would-be homeowners can come by and see what the Golankas have done, and they gladly open their doors.

The Golanka home reflects a real love of wood in the architecture, both inside and out. "We've always enjoyed more of a natural look. Even in our old home we had done a lot of work and put a lot of wood into it. We enjoy the warmth that it brings, the entire atmosphere. This was just a natural progression of that. When you are that involved, or that much in love with that look, this just becomes the natural progression to that," Conrad said. "There's no drywall in our house. The house is all either log or tongue-and-groove knotty pine. Like I said, you can custom do these things to whatever your taste is."

Given the task to do over, Conrad said he'd only change one thing. "I would have direct access from the garage into the basement," he said. "As the seasons change we move a lot of things either into the garage or the basement. Right now you have to come into the house to do it. For instance, we keep a lot of the pool stuff in the basement in the winter, so it would be more convenient."

However, he quickly shrugs that off as a minor inconvenience. "Our hardest part of the day is getting up in the morning and leaving. Especially when the snow is falling, you just want to throw some more wood on the fire and stay in the house."

Conrad and Mary Golanka with their daughter, Cathy.

First Floor

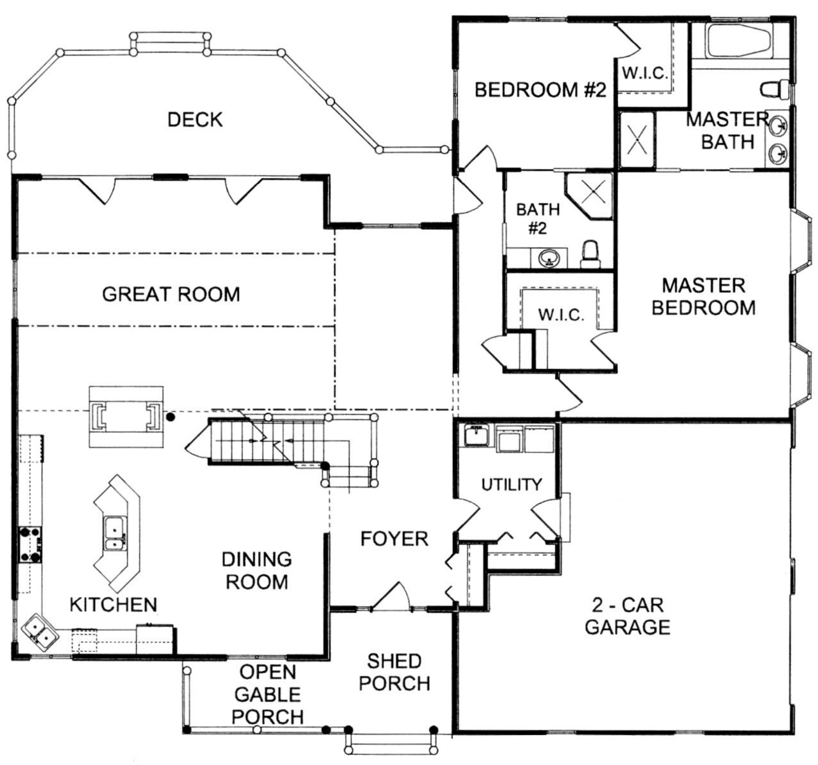

Second Floor

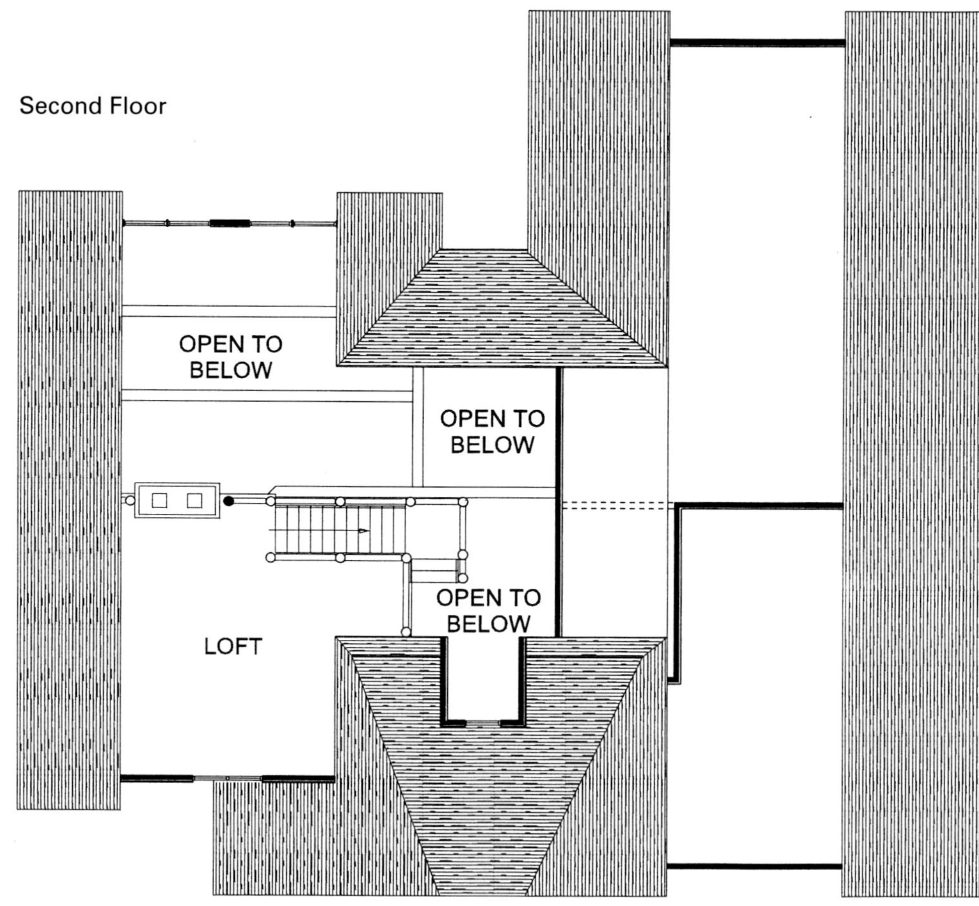

This home looks like it occupies a rural site, but it is only half an hour from downtown Chicago, says homeowner Conrad Golanka. "It has a country feel, but you're really not in the country. It was a nice compromise for us – close enough to work, close enough to the city, far enough from the city – it's got a lot of good points about it." This rear elevation shot shows the elevated deck, and the wide, open staircase placed off the great room so there wouldn't be a railing blocking the view.

34

Opposite page:
This home has a unique palette of colors, from the dark grey for the mortar and a lot of burgundy, including the front door. Green shingles and Pella windows complete the look, one so pretty that cars passing by slow down, the owners say. Mary Golanka created this beautiful entryway garden to greet visitors.

This page:
The massive, two-way fireplace commands a central location, warming the great room as well as the kitchen and dining areas. It's actually made of Cultured Stone®, a concrete that "is not nearly as heavy as using natural stone, and it doesn't require all of the reinforcing that natural stone does. It gives you the same look," Conrad said. The family spends most of their time in the great room or the kitchen, he added.

Nine-foot patio doors were topped by step or varied-height windows. Together they introduce a lot of light into the great room.

This home started out as a ranch with very high ceilings, but during the building process the family changed their mind and added the loft. It's actually as simple as the addition of a stairwell and some flooring, says Jan Koepsell of Expedition Log Homes. These kind of mid-process changes are common, too, she added. The Golankas are glad they made the decision. Before she went off to college, "My daughter and her friends used to use it a lot. Unfortunately she's away at college right now. It gets used during the holidays. The adults tend to congregate, and the kids disappear up there the entire time they are here. It's a nice place for them to remove themselves and amuse themselves."

"The kitchen tends to be a nice place to gravitate, which is why we had the island put in," said the homeowner. "My daughter's friends would hang around the kitchen and make themselves something to eat. Then they'd plop down and sit by the fire." The dining room is open to the kitchen, and a small half wall blocks the refrigerator and creates a small niche. Again, the family's love of wood is evidenced by the logs used to face their island and knotty pine cabinetry. Easy maintenance grey slate tile underlines the area.

The home's burgundy and grey theme was carried over in the dining area, with accent touches and a rug. Mary took her cue from an image she saw in a magazine, and carefully chose paints and textiles to create the look she wanted.

In a small nook off the entryway, a home office is defined as separate from the great room by a change in the ceiling height.

The master bedroom was furnished with a four-poster bed and other more traditional pieces. The master suite, with the exception of a carpeted floor, is wood from top to bottom.

Family Spread

Jim and Kita Goodson planned their home for many years. They always knew they'd build on the 140-acre farm where Jim grew up, and after vacationing in Breckenridge, Colorado, they knew they wanted a log home.

"We planned for about six years, gathering ideas," Jim said. The result has been fantastic.

"We had some people come up from Texas who wanted to build a house and they asked what we'd change if we did it over again. We really couldn't come up with anything. It has everything we've ever dreamed about having. Never say never, but I don't think we'll ever move from here."

The home has a lot of areas that the Goodson family enjoys. In fact, Jim said, they are utilizing the whole house. "There are different areas and we enjoy them all. We're utilizing the whole house. We're not actually out on the deck as much as you'd think. You don't really have to go out on the deck to get the same views."

Jim and Kita Goodson, with Josh and Meg.

LODGE

Opposite page, and left:
A big, open-gable porch provides a welcome for visitors to the Goodson family home in Iowa, and a shed porch next to it provides a shady place to relax. Just beyond, a goldfish pond provides splashes of color, and a waterway running under the entrance walk provides natural music.

The rear elevation of the home shows off the wall of glass, where a deck tops a walk-out basement, and two-stories of glass rise to illuminate the great room inside, and reveal views of the family's rich resources outside. Owners Jim and Kita Goodson have dedicated parts of their property to a conservation program, and there is lots of wildlife to be glimpsed.

Burgundy wallpaper in the entryway matches the carbonite Pella™ entry doors. The kitchen is just off the entry, behind the log support post.

The great room faces the outside with two walls of glass and one of stone. The stone surrounding the fireplace is actually Cultured Stone®, a concrete product that closely mimics the real thing.

A deck beyond the great room is a great draw, but with such an expanse of glass inside, owner Jim Goodson says they enjoy the same great views from inside as from out. A waterfall effect was created for the windows, incorporating quarter rounds with traditional standard windows. This image also shows the small balcony off the office upstairs.

Gingham, wallpaper borders, and wood finishes reflect the casual, country atmosphere of the Goodson family home. The Cultured Stone® on the fireplace is repeated on the face of the kitchen island. A built-in TV tops the oven.

A home office with balcony includes built-in cabinets that match the kitchen treatment.

A woodstove keeps a sunroom cozy in the winter.

The master bedroom with amazing furniture utilizing different stains and woods, proving that everything doesn't have to match in a log home.

Vacation Every Day

Linda and Tony Em fell in love with round-top windows as they studied pictures of other log homes. A two-story wall of windows backs their great room, and a repeat of the motif was carried over to the master suite. A gazebo type bump-out is their dining room.

Linda and Tony Em had longed for a log home on the lake for many years. They rented cabins for their vacations, studied magazines, and filed away favorite pictures. Now they feel as though they're on vacation every day.

Semi-retired, they have their home on Lake Murray, South Carolina. "It feels very peaceful and relaxing and comfortable," Linda said of their new life.

Linda said she studied the log home magazines for many years. "I just cut pictures out that I liked, and said 'I want that, that, and that'."

The priorities included "the stone fireplace," she said, "and the round-top windows. We wanted partial log inside, with a lot of drywall. In the great room and dining room I wanted some log, but we wanted some brightness to it, too."

Because they plan on spending the rest of their days in this home, they wanted their master suite downstairs, and two bedrooms and a full bath off the loft for guests and family that come. "We really just stay downstairs all the time," she said.

The front elevation of this home was kept quite simple, with small windows. Because the home is on a lake, the windows were lavished on the other side of the home to capture the views.

A shot of the deck shows off the log structure. The siding is flat-on-flat with interlocking, hand-crafted saddle notch corners.

The great room was finished in drywall, with a bank of glass topped by quarter-round windows. These shots show the log post that supports the loft, as well as the matching logs used on the stairs and railing. "We spend most of the time in the great room," said Linda Em. "You can look out the windows and see the fireplace and the TV – everything."

The dining room sits in a small bump-out with its own vaulted ceiling characterized by log rafters and knotty pine ceiling panels. "We use it every day," the owner says.

The kitchen includes a beautiful bay window, which Linda Em accented with hand-painted stenciling.

The master bedroom repeats the same quarter-round windows and vaulted ceiling found in the great room, only on a smaller scale.

The dining room sits in a small bump-out with its own vaulted ceiling characterized by log rafters and knotty pine ceiling panels. "We use it every day," the owner says.

Interior Designs

"It's so much fun to decorate," says Julie Galdi of her log home. "It's so much different than decorating a conventional home. You can be whimsical and do whatever you want."

Julie and her husband Mario built themselves a second home near the Windham Mountain ski resorts of New York.

The couple had always wanted a log cabin, Julie said, and had kept their eyes opened for years waiting for an opportunity. "When we found this place we jumped on it, because it's so conveniently located," she said. "It's under two hours from our permanent residence in New Jersey, so we go every weekend. If my husband has off, or my youngest son has off from school, we go for longer. He's on a ski team, so he needs to be up there every weekend in the winter to practice.

"We've always loved the look of a log cabin. When you're in there, you just feel like you're on vacation. No one we really know has ever had a log home.

The Galdi's have been in their second home for three years now, and the compliments just pour in. Friends and family admire their home, and, because it was so beautifully decorated, it has been featured in magazines.

"People call who saw my name in a magazine article. They want to get this," Julie marvels. Naturally, she's proud of the home.

"My husband was the general contractor, so he really planned and did most of the work. This was his first attempt at a cabin. His main business is mechanical contracting. But he built our home in New Jersey and a few other small projects. I think that this is the nicest thing he's ever done."

Julie did the décor. "We tried to do a lot of unique things. I did a lot of online purchasing. I'd never really purchased things online before we did this house. There are a lot of places out West, and we ordered so much furniture and lighting fixtures through the Internet. That really worked out well. Then a lot of the other pieces were antiques converted. The bar is made out of real old barn board. And all the railings were done by hand."

The design of the home suits them beautifully. "The main floor is like one giant room – the kitchen, dining room, and bar setup. That's my absolute favorite place to be. I love to cook. You're just right on top of everyone. We have a lot of people who like to come up and visit. Everyone is just kind of on top of each other, which is nice. It's one big, wide-open area. We did that on purpose. And the view from that area is just spectacular. You see two big mountains, two ski areas."

Julie and Mario Galdi.

FIRST FLOOR

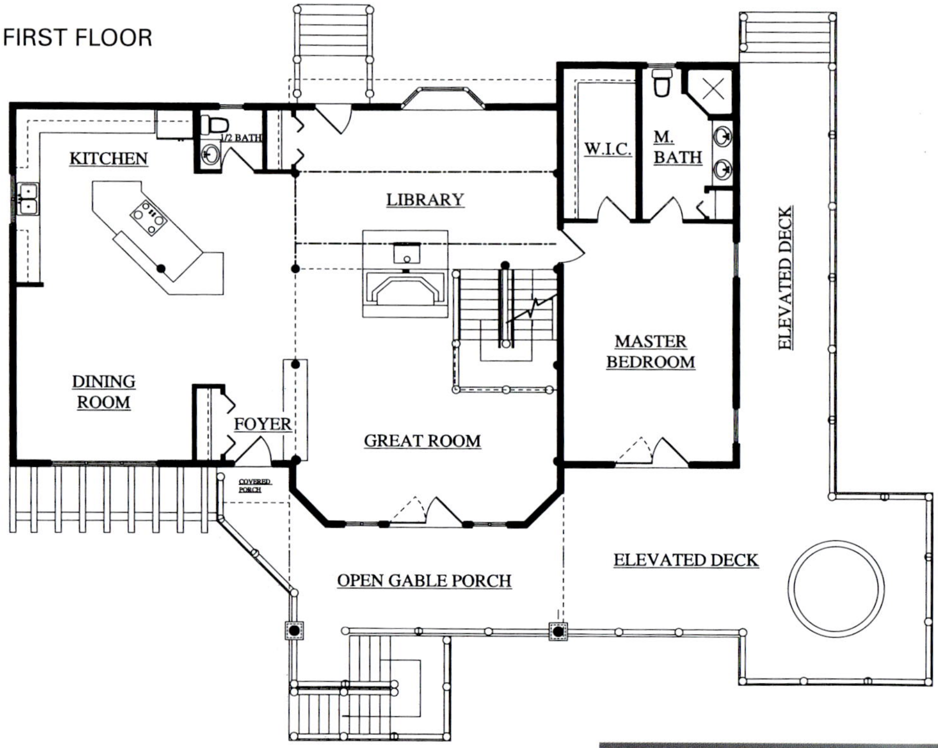

KITCHEN
1/2 BATH
LIBRARY
W.I.C.
M. BATH
DINING ROOM
FOYER
GREAT ROOM
MASTER BEDROOM
ELEVATED DECK
COVERED PORCH
OPEN GABLE PORCH
ELEVATED DECK

SECOND FL OOR

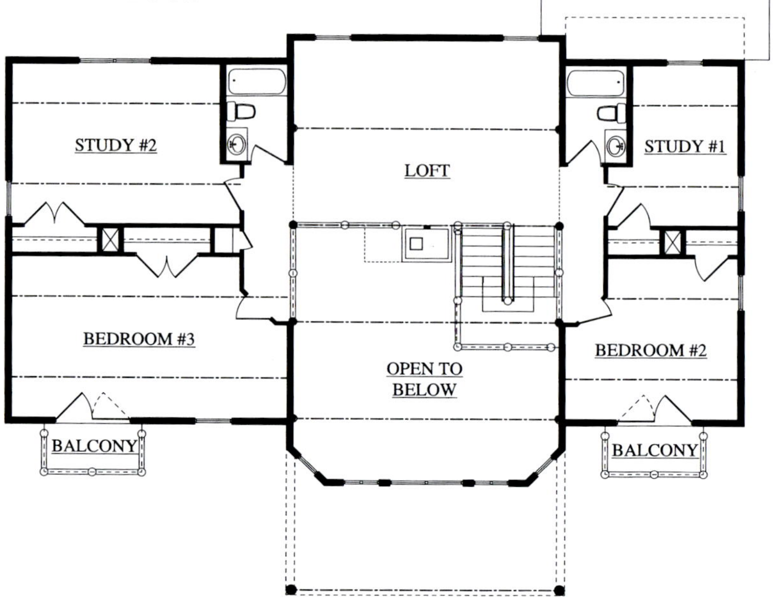

STUDY #2
LOFT
STUDY #1
BEDROOM #3
OPEN TO BELOW
BEDROOM #2
BALCONY
BALCONY

Lots of glass and double doors characterize the dramatic entrance from a private drive, revealing the two-story open gabled roof with tie-beam, king post, and diagonals, replicated in the bump-ups over the second-floor bedrooms.

A little gazebo provides an architectural element on the balcony, sheltering a hot tub where the family enjoys the view during all four seasons. Cedar logs were used to side this home, creating an easy maintenance exterior.

Stone pillars support the roof posts. A garage is tucked under the deck.

The open kitchen plan allows Julie Galdi access to family and guests, as well as the ability to provide big meals with efficiency. A spaghetti faucet on the wall behind the stove is an asset for a woman who loves to cook. The pot rack over the island is handy as well as decorative.

A wood-burning stove warms the dining room, and seems appropriate next to a wall of timber logs with chinking. A lowered drywall ceiling with log rafters adds intimacy to the space, located just off the soaring great room.

A loft overlooks the great room with its massive fireplace. Timber log with chinking faces the entryway walls, then transitions to half logs for the rest of the home interior. The king post and rafters with diagonals that greet visitors as they drive up are repeated inside the entryway.

A corner bar area is located near the kitchen and dining area, tucked under the loft, furnished with a window seat and saddle stools.

A gaming area was created in the loft. The owners' sense of humor is reflected in their *American Gothic* caricatures. The loft provides an opportunity to observe the skip-peeled logs, where the logs were peeled to retain some cambium-layer for a multi-toned, rustic appearance.

The master bedroom was faced with timber logs and chinking. In the bath, a glass shower creates an open feeling in the room.

A powder room was finished with timber logs and chinking, as well as wonderful furnishings researched and purchased by Julie Galdi.

A guest bedroom was finished with painted walls and knotty pine wainscoting that matches the ceiling panels.

Decades in the Making

Sometimes it starts with a specific vision, this one of standing in a wilderness setting with a 360-degree view of nature. It was Jodi's dream to live in a log home in the middle of the woods, a home that also had a special place that would fulfill that vision. Along the way, husband Steve shared the dream and the result is a 2,424 square foot, very traditional full round butt-and-pass corner log home with three bedrooms and two baths nestled amid twenty-six acres in North Central Wisconsin.

"I wanted to see all around, like being in the middle of the woods," says Jodi. "I'm really big into nature and wildlife. I'm critter crazy, so the room is wonderful!"

Jodi incorporated antler chandeliers in the dining area and even had metal bear paw prints imbedded in the walkway up to the front porch that runs the length of the home.

The porch is another important detail. "We had seen where front porches can tend to sway," she says, "so we had cement poured and then it was stamped and painted to look like planks. A lot of people are surprised when they find that out, because it looks so authentic."

Practicality led to another attractive detail. Caulking could be seen in the tongue-and-groove joints of several interior beams. Jodi wasn't about to let that detract from the home's important details. She bought decorative rope and the builder used it to wrap the joints so that the caulk seams were hidden.

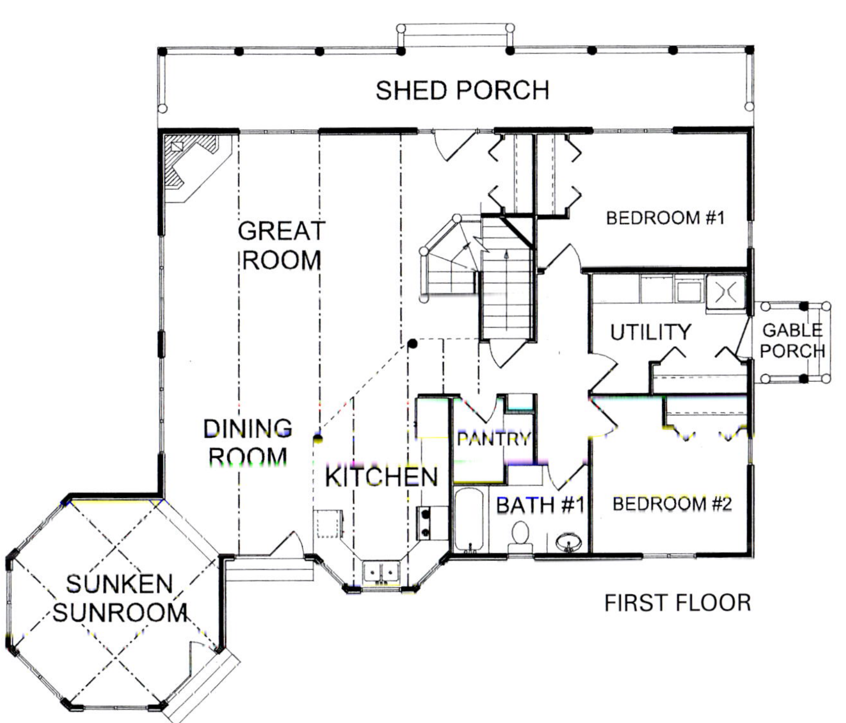

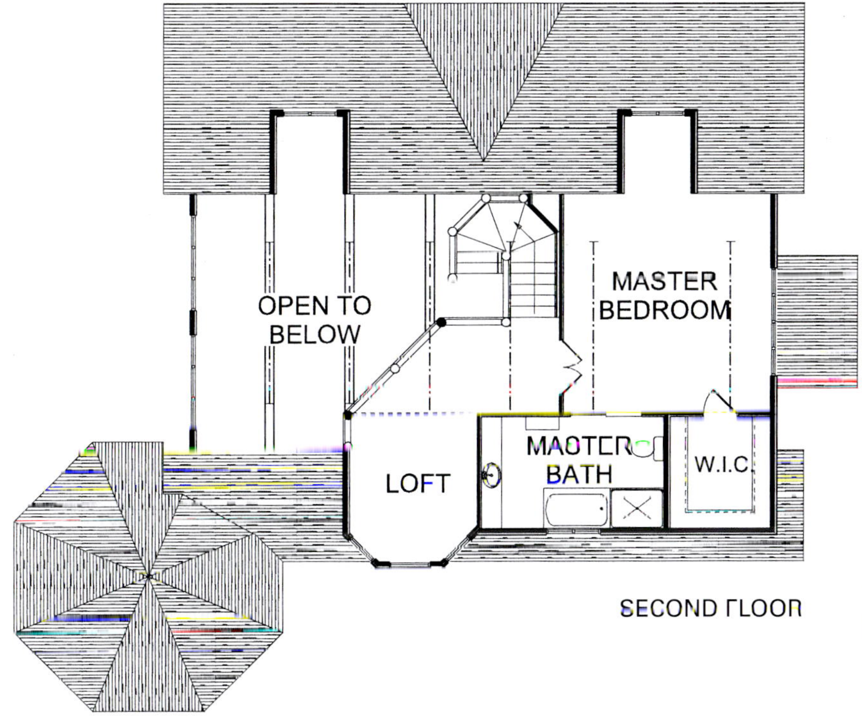

A little pizzazz is created for this log cabin home with copper flashing on the roof, as well as copper gutters and downspouts. The front porch was finished with a stamped concrete surface that makes the surface look just like wood decking, but requires very little maintenance. Stones and stumps help define parking areas within this natural setting.

A rear elevation shot shows the octagonal, sunken sunroom off the dining room. It also shows the bump-out that provides just a little extra space in their kitchen, and an attractive nook for the sink area. The roofline in the back combines the upper level and loft as it blends into a shed dormer on the backside – a really nice look. In the wooded backyard, stumps have been gathered and placed round a firepit for cool autumn get-togethers.

A bear announces one's arrival to a true cabin-style home. The stairs and landing were finished in logs, and contribute character to both entryway and the adjacent great room.

The great room blends living spaces including a gathering area, the dining room, and the kitchen together within the glow of a great bank of graduated windows. A corner fireplace is visible to the entire great room area, including the kitchen.

An efficient kitchen keeps the work areas and appliances close at hand, while a pantry nearby provides plenty of additional storage. With the dining area close at hand, the entire setup saves energy and time for a busy family. The dining room was furnished with log-style chairs and table for informal entertaining. The kitchen island incorporates the support post, in character with the rest of the home.

A window seat and home office are among the amenities of a lofty hideaway.

The sunny octagonal sunroom is a favorite getaway, set off from the kitchen and dining area and serving as a cozy nook with a sense of connectedness to the woods beyond. Exposed log rafters draw attention to the ceiling above.

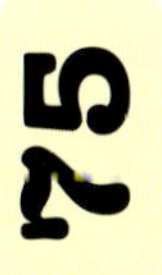

The master suite spreads out across the second floor of the home, while the children's rooms were kept downstairs. Above it all, the homeowners enjoy a large bath and walk in closet. They can step out onto a loft and command a view of the living areas below.

Farm and Family

Homeowner Jill Isken says she loves her home, "Most of all because it looks so American, and its very cozy and comfortable – a place to relax in." Jill and her husband, George, planned their cozy home for keeps. They've got big plans for their ten-acre spread, including some livestock. In fact, that's a real chicken you can see on the front porch steps.

The dream started before the happy homesteaders met. "Before George and I got married, I had been on my horse walking around and I saw this beautiful log home. I just loved it so much, I said if 'I ever build a home I'll build a log home'."

Jill and George Isken relax on their front deck, furnished with a log swing perfect for two.

Married, George and Jill broke ground on some land owned by George's family, out in the country, near Lake Michigan just north of Milwaukee. George's daughter lives next door, and two additional acres have been sold to his son, "so we're surrounded by family out here," Jill says. And they love their home.

Jill spends most of her time in the kitchen, she said, and she couldn't ask for a better workspace. "Everything's at your fingertips – it's efficient, yet big enough to walk around in. I like that the great room and dining room are all in one area. You can spend your time in the kitchen doing all the things you do, but still watch TV or talk to people sitting in the room." More importantly, she shares in the view of the lake from the great room.

They wanted to keep the house small but inviting, with room for entertaining. It's also small enough that the woodstove in the corner of the great room is almost all they need to heat their home through a Wisconsin winter. "The gas is just for backup," Jill said.

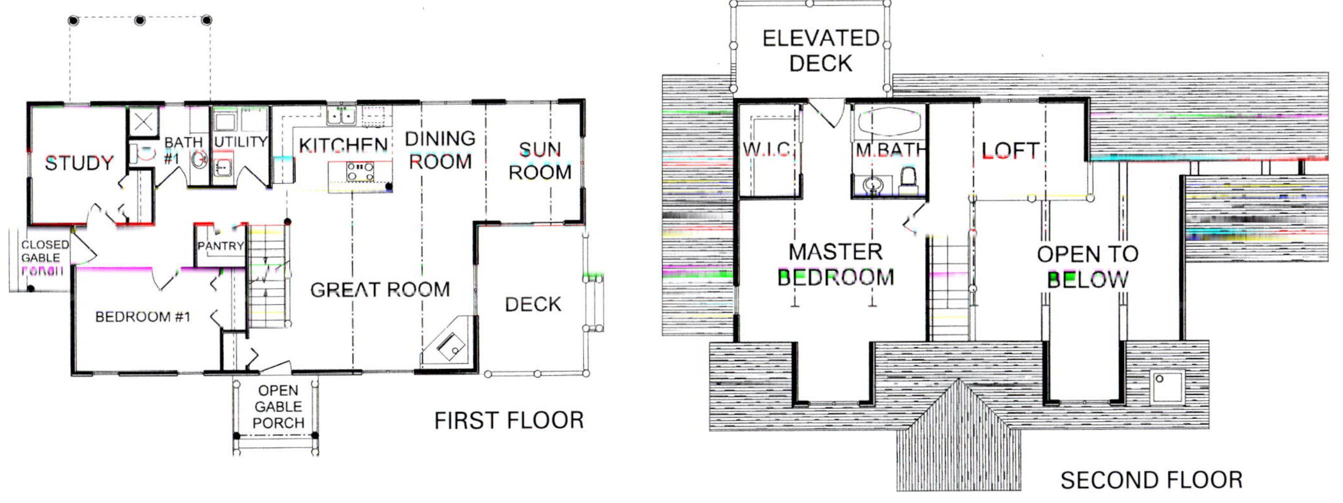

A beautiful entryway recalls the log cabin Jill once came across when out horseback riding.

Aesthetically they chose the "Cabin log," a thinner log for the exterior, trimmed with half-logs for a complementary effect that really makes the windows and door openings pop.

Huge tie beams put on quite a display in the great room, but it's not all grandeur. Comfort was incorporated with deep-cushion furnishings and favorite things all around.

Window ledges in the sunroom allow the Iskens to display their collectibles, and they also adorned the tops of their tie beams.

Homeowner Jill Isken says she doesn't mind her kitchen chores so much, since this space is efficient work-wise, and open to the world beyond. She can watch TV or talk to people elsewhere in the house as she works.

A master suite on the second floor includes a spacious bath, a walk-in closet, and a secluded loft area. There's lots of architectural eye candy among the eaves, from both the roof angles and the contrast of wood ceilings and paneling with white drywall.

Daily Blessing

Five years after moving in, Jack and Judy McCarthy are still in love with their new house. "We just feel so blessed," Judy said. "We say prayers of thanksgiving every night that we have been able to live in it and enjoy it."

Judy grew up in Northeast Minnesota, and introduced her husband to the area. "My husband and I are nature-type people. We love the outdoors, fishing, and hunting. When I introduced him to the area about twenty years ago he fell in love with it. We camped on the property for about fifteen years with the idea that some day we would build a log home," she said.

When it came time to build, they knew what they wanted. "It was our design. When we built the house we built it with the idea that we would share it with a lot of people. Our family comes up a lot and we enjoy entertaining." This is the first log home they've owned. "We sat down and just kind of piecemeal started putting things down as to what we would like and what we wanted. "When we took it to Expedi-

Jack and Judy McCarthy (seated) asked to be pictured with their builders, Mike and Don of Aune & Keister Construction in Cook, Minnesota. "Without them we would never have had our dream home. They were great guys to work with, and they did it from start to finish – they did everything," Judy stated.

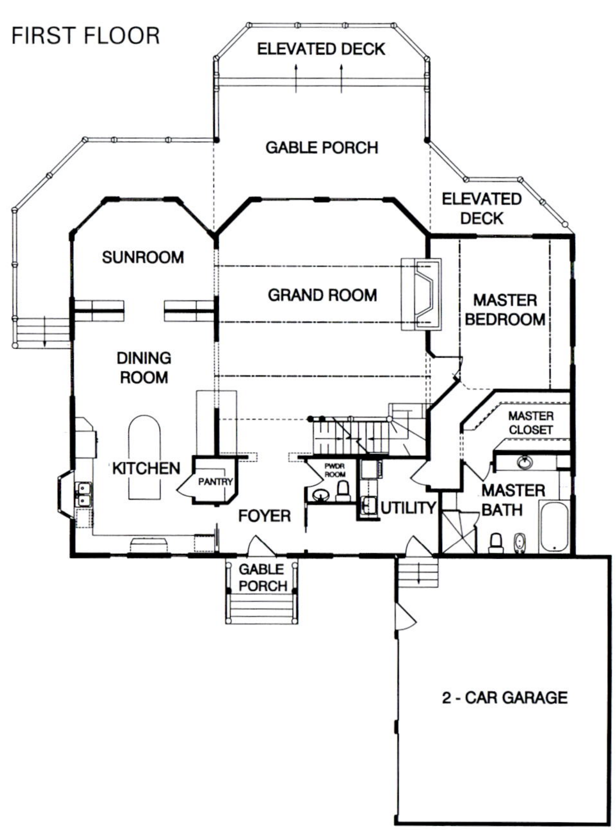

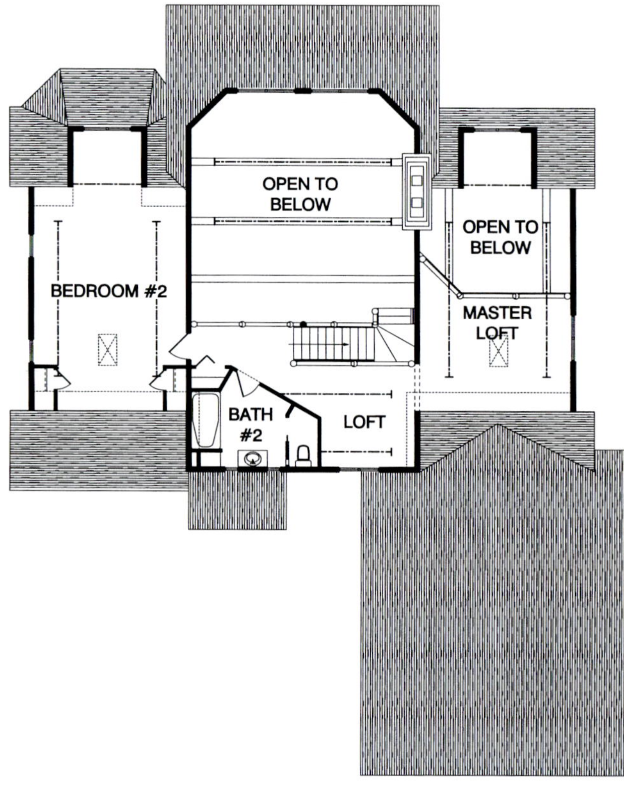

tion, they took our ideas and put them down and made it structurally sound. Basically it was our plan."

"It's a fun house," she says of the result. "I love everything. Often we have said to people when they say 'what would you do differently.' I say nothing. It's comfortable, it's warm. We put in radiant heating, and it's very, very comfortable heatwise. We have a half-log system with six inches of insulation, and then on the inside it gave us the opportunity to do any kind of finish – we have knotty pine and sheetrock. We have a stone fireplace and stone on the outside. My husband did all the stonework on the outside of our house, which is really pretty."

The McCarthys were one of the first clients for Expedition Log Homes. "We were so pleased with our representative, Jay Enderson and the company and the product, that once our house was built we decided we would be an associate," Judy said. So now the McCarthy's assist as representatives in the Northeast Minnesota territory.

A small portico welcomes visitors to the home of Jack and Judy McCarthy in Northern Minnesota. This rural retreat is frequented by friends and family, and the door is often opened to prospective home builders who want to visit a beautiful log cabin.

Besides a pretty entry, the front of the house isn't that exciting. The homeowners chose to put their air conditioning units and garage doors in the front in order to preserve the pristine Northern Minnesota lakefront that backs their property.

Log beams and a loft area overlook the great room, made warm and cozy with half-log and knotty pine paneling. A stone shelf allowed the big-screen TV to be incorporated with the fireplace, a beautiful way to incorporate the large appliance.

A sunroom off the dining area creates a wonderful, cozy nook, in command of the view, and in proximity to kitchen and great room.

A lot of color and paint was incorporated into the kitchen, giving it a homey air.

The stairway included character logs for the rail system and the custom-cut steps.

The large guest bedroom and guest bath were created upstairs for frequent visitors.

The master bedroom was furnished with log furniture, handcrafted by Jay Enderson of Moosehead Log Rails and Furniture. The master bedroom has a cathedral ceiling and includes a private loft area, lit by a round-top window. The loft is a wonderful escape, furnished with a love seat, reading lamp, and bookshelf.

Year-round Vacation

A summer cottage near Dowagiac, Michigan, provided a wonderful getaway for Dottie and Frank Petriko and their children for more than thirty years. They bought a small lakefront cottage there and, because they ran their own travel agency, they were able to find flexible time to extend their weekends there.

"The travel industry is really changing, and we decided maybe it was time to retire. I suggested 'maybe we should retire here and build a log home,' and my husband didn't argue," Dottie says. And so it happened.

"We've always admired log homes," Dottie says about the first part of their decision. "It has a very 'lodge-y' look to it. Something about a log home, it's warm, it's solid. It has a very homey feeling."

More than six years of visiting the site and spending time in the cottage helped to determine the final shape of their log home. "The old cottage had a huge porch that overlooked the lake and we practically lived out there," Dottie said. "So this house has two porches where we spend a lot of time. We put a lot of bird food out and we love to watch the birds."

Next on the list was the kitchen/great room, because the couple loves to cook and entertain. "We got to design the kitchen from scratch," Dottie said. "We have a large island, which is great for serving buffet style or for people gathering around. But I also have a second island – a butcher block, and that's my favorite accessory in the kitchen. Because we're retired we have a lot more time to cook or to entertain. The dining room flows nicely into the great room, it just lends itself nicely to entertaining. We like theme parties. For instance, we went to Thailand in the spring, so we came home and found all the ingredients and made a big Thai dinner for all of our friends."

Then there are the children and grandchildren who still love to spend time at the family retreat, and that helped determine sleeping accommodations. "Since this is our retirement home, for us it was important to have all of our living space for my husband and I on one floor. We have two guest bedrooms upstairs, and each has a bathroom. We feel when we're here that we're on vacation every day.

"Dottie is a woman with a real knack for making a place feel like home," marvels Jan Koepsell of Expedition Log Homes. The Petrikos "placed their order in August, and in less than twelve months they had their house ordered, up, and decorated just as you see it in these pictures. A lot of cute decorating things, with lots of antiques appropriate to the cabin-on-the-lake feeling. It feels like family, and yet elegant," Koepsell said.

"We lived in a suburb of Chicago, a very urban area that we lived in all of our lives, and then we moved to a very rural area," Dorothy said. "When we come back here after visiting our kids in the city, there's a certain sense of peace that we feel here. We love it here because in the summers we're on a lake. We have two children with families, and they love spending time up here all year long. We love the summer because of boating and swimming, and we love snowmobiling in the winter. We're just half a mile from the state trails. We could go to Canada if we wanted. In the fall the kids come up to pick apple and pumpkins. We really love all four seasons."

Dottie and Frank Petriko.

FIRST FLOOR

SECOND FLOOR

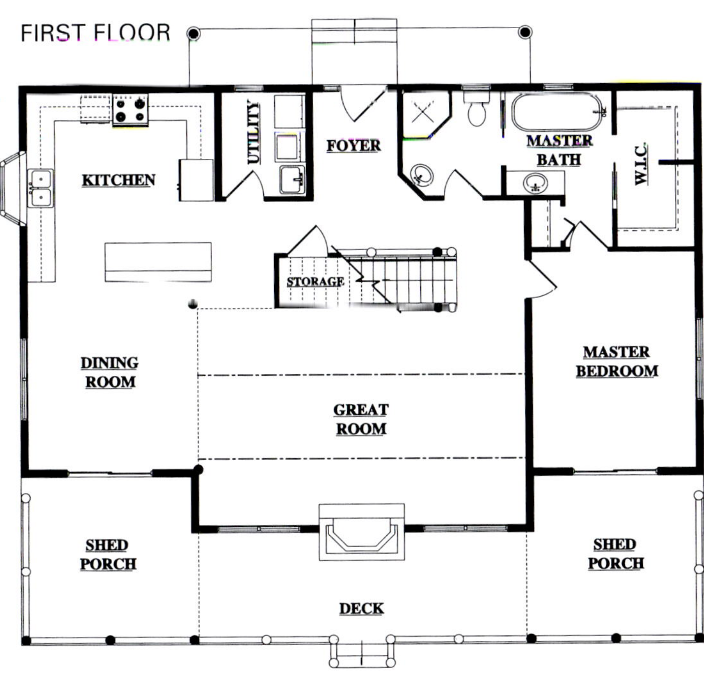

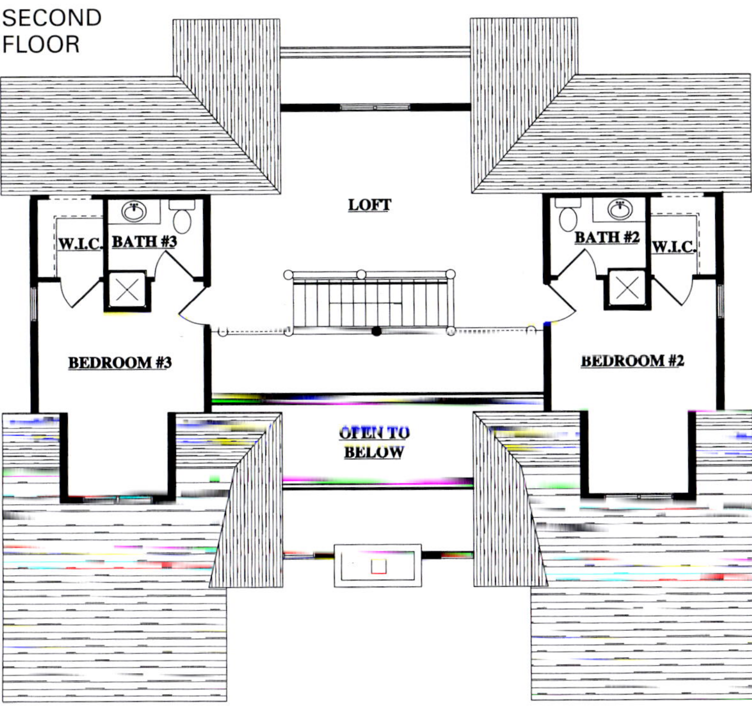

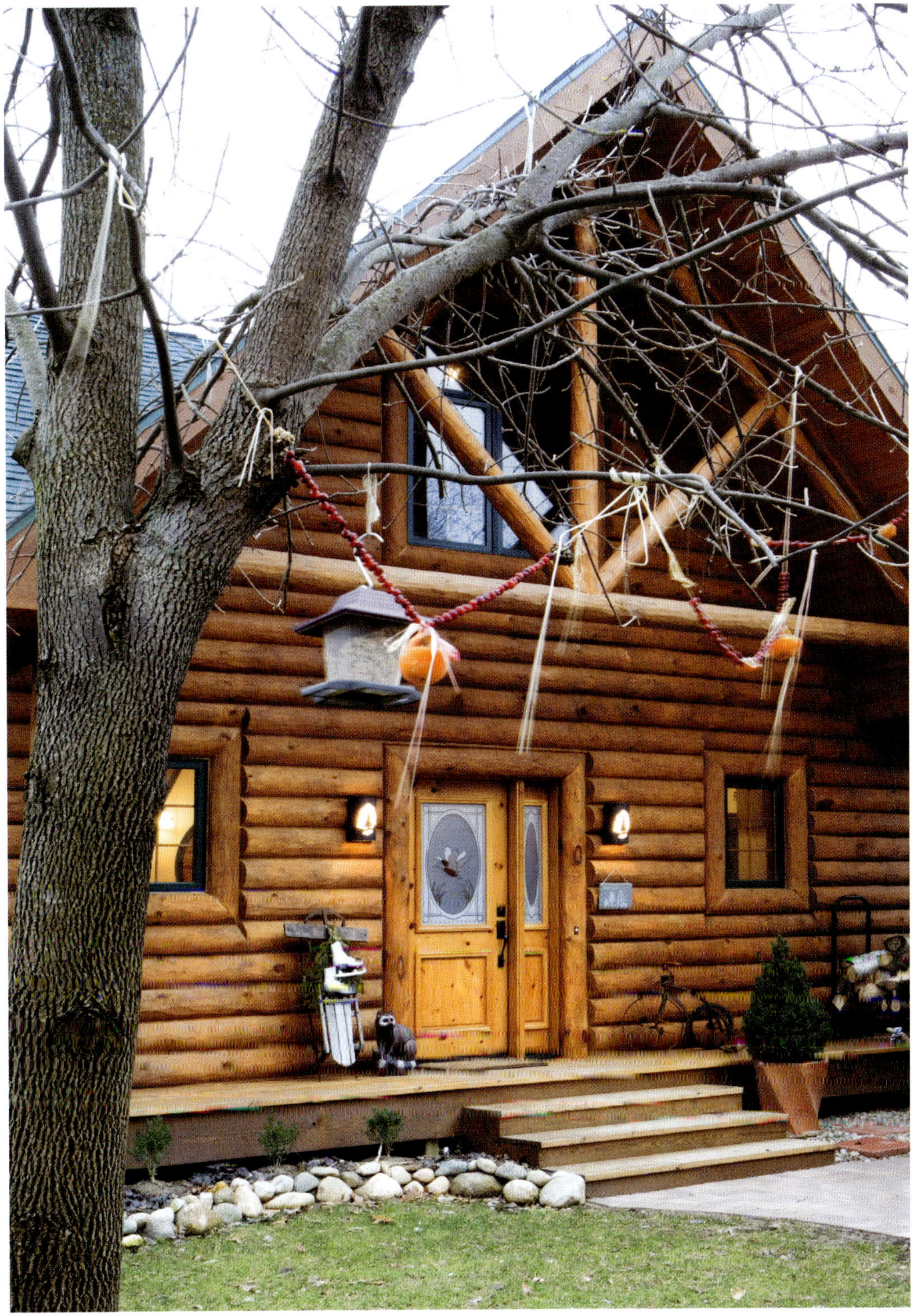

A beautiful, two-story portico invites visitors to this home, the log king-post truss proudly displayed. The owners clad their home in eight-inch logs.

Located on a beautiful lake near Kalamazoo, Michigan, these homeowners wanted to take full advantage of their view. The back of their house includes wonderful picture windows, sliding doors, and two screened-in porches, since mosquitoes tend to summer here as well.

In the kitchen, a lowered ceiling of hammered copper supports a pot hangar. A character post was incorporated and forms a terminus for the island work area. Wallpaper, paint, and accessories personalize and add warmth to this kitchen.

Quarter-round windows and a double set of sliding doors flank a great stone fireplace and minimize the separation of interior and outside. "Flying geese" emphasize the lofty heights among the tie beams.

"Cabin logs" were chosen for the interior walls. The larger half-log siding trim around the door really stands out against the thinner logs.

Antiques and unique furnishings prove that a log cabin can be the perfect setting for all types of décor. Sliding doors make it easy to move the meal outside, weather permitting.

The Petriko's wanted to stay connected to the outdoors, even in the master bedroom, where a glass slider opens to a screened porch.

A loft area makes for a great getaway for this retired couple, but also adds the luxury of some private living space when the grown children and their families come to visit.

Grandchildren are welcome, so much so that a miniature clawfoot tub was installed to indulge the little guests.

High in the Mountains

Immediately following his dental internship, former Ohio State student Larry Warren found himself assigned to the Fort Apache Indian Reservation in the White Mountains of Arizona working for the Indian Health Services. A newfound love brought him and wife Donna back time and again, and they've finally realized their dream of a second home in this high-altitude wonderland.

They are ecstatic about their new two-acre property. "We just love it up here," Donna said. "The property has a really good view overlooking the meadow. We wanted our home to look out over this view from the dining room, family room, and bedroom. It is picturesque."

"There're elk out there every night," Larry said. "We have two acres, one in the trees where the house is, the other below with a meadow and stream. The location is great."

Living in Scottsdale, the Warren's find themselves marveling anew every time they get away to visit their forest home. "It's the largest continuous stand of ponderosa pine in the country," Larry said. "At 8,500 feet we're right on the edge of where the pine at high elevations turns to aspen. We have some aspen on our property, as well as spruce and fir."

Donna points out that they designed their home to sit behind two ponderosa pines, "so that when we walked to the front door we walked between them." Unfortunately, due to drought, both trees died under attack by beetles. Still, they preserved them by having the trunks carved. Trent Penrod of Pinetop, Arizona, came out with a chain saw and turned the smaller stump into an eight-foot bear. The other has a bear emerging out of the top, a baby bear with his 'behind' coming out of the back of the tree, and two raccoons sitting in the backside of the tree. "It was really fun to do and we were able to keep part of the trees that way," Larry said.

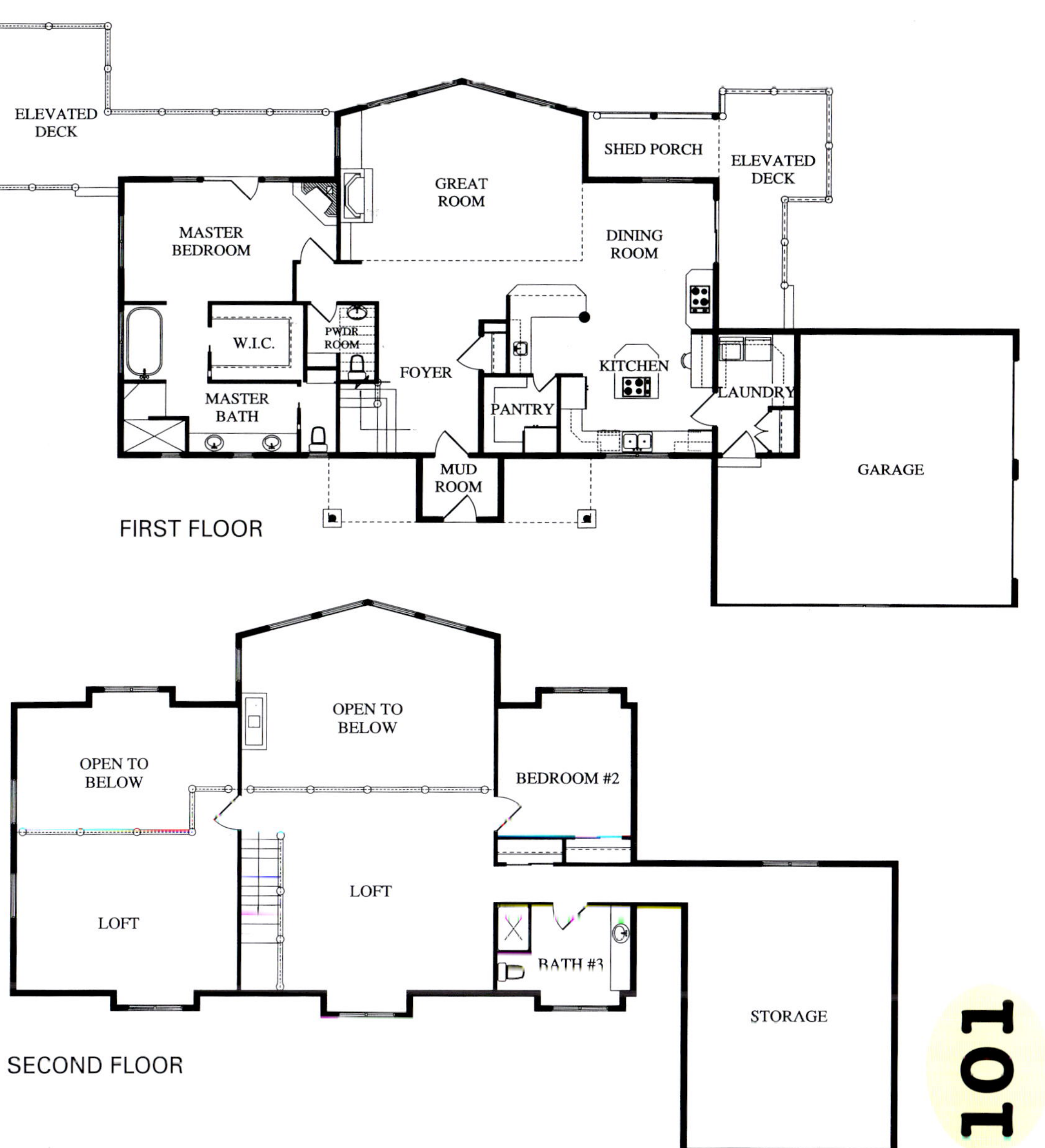

The Warren's designed their second home to include a home office, but "we try not to work there," they both say. Their goal is a place to get away from all that. "Eventually we'll probably spend more time here than in Scottsdale," Donna said. "So if there's a necessity we can work out of here." Larry notes that they haven't hooked up to the Internet yet, and are in no hurry to do so.

"This is our escape place where we come to get away from the pressures of every day life," Larry said emphatically.

This second home backs up to a forest in the White Mountains of Arizona, while the windows of all the main living areas look out over a lovely meadow.

The loss of two ponderosa pines to beetle infestation was a disappointment to the homeowners, who'd built the home so that their approach to the front door passed between these great beauties. The trees are even more remarkable in memoriam, however, with the addition of some artful carving and finishing. Because it was placed on the side of a mountain, you have to go downhill a little bit to get to the front door. A bump-out at the entry gives an interesting architectural effect, with the twin rows of butt and pass log corners.

A small extension of the deck creates a nice gathering area for seating and dining al fresco.

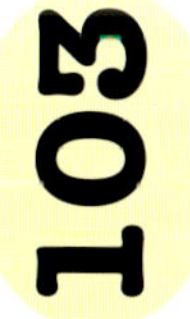

The Warrens find themselves spending most of their time in the great room. "When people come in here the first thing they pickup on is the open space, and the beauty of the log, the window," Donna said. The fireplace in the great room has propane to start natural logs. The vaulted ceiling rises twenty-two feet.

Furnishings further define this mountain lodge, with the profile of ponderosa pines an integral part of the dining set, overlooked by an antler chandelier.

The Warrens distressed the floor themselves during the construction process, using tire chains and hammers before the finishing process. "We wanted it to feel older," they explained. The support beam in the kitchen is one of their favorite features in the home, defining the log character of their mountain getaway.

The Warrens initially planned to create a room upstairs, but the contractor asked "why would you put a wall up there that would hide the beautiful beams, logs, and window?" Following his advice, the room is now Donna's favorite. "It is now a large loft and looks down over the great room, and the window wall. It's really a pretty setting," she said.

The master and guest room are both fed sunlight and view by a generous allowance of windows. In addition, a bunkroom over the garage easily accommodates more than a dozen people, making this a wonderful retreat for large groups of family and friends.

Decades of Dreaming

Daphne Livingstone dreamed of living in a log home for better than thirty years. From the time she and her husband, Tim, married, they talked of someday building this dream home. "It's something we wanted to do the whole time we were married," she said.

The delay, she said, was the result of a sensible plan to wait until they could own the house, without the house owning them. They carefully researched what they were getting themselves into. "A lot of people don't realize the maintenance a log home requires in order to stay beautiful," Daphne said. She and her husband just spent half their summer weekends re-staining the exterior logs, a very physical process that, though they've enjoyed it, they may hire younger helpers to do the next time around, in about five years.

"If you want to have pride in your home, you have to keep up on more things," she said. "Because of the research we did we've been very pro-active. It's not a chore; this is what we wanted. It's nothing the average person couldn't do," she says of the work. Their pride in ownership shows. That's one of the fringe benefits of working hard to maintain the pristine condition of the house. "I enjoy being outside working on my house, and people stopping by to tell me how beautiful my house is."

As a young girl, Daphne's family used to vacation in cabins. "Now every morning when I wake up I feel like I'm back in that cabin. I like the fact that, when I'm in my house I always feel like I'm on vacation. Does that sound silly?"

After being assured that other log home owners have said virtually the same thing, Daphne goes on to state that another favorite aspect of her home is: "it is what we designed. It's what we put down on paper and now we're there!"

Like other log home owners, Daphne reiterates that "There's just something special about all that wood. It's the homey feeling – a good, comfortable feeling."

Tim, Daphne, and Tim Livingstone.

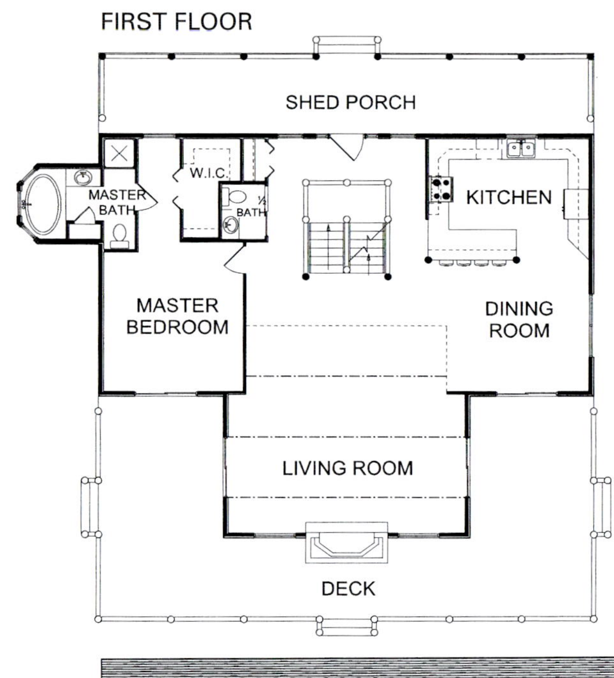

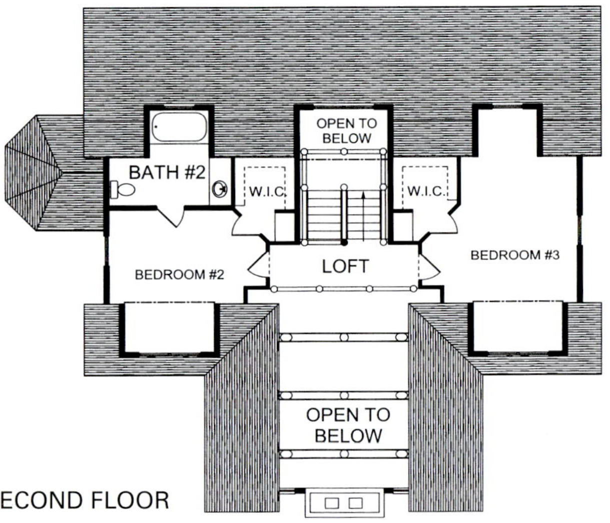

Daphne and Tim well remember the morning in October when Roger Wade showed up to photograph their log cabin in southwestern Pennsylvania. After a string of gorgeous, balmy autumn days, they awoke to find four inches of snow covering the lawn and house. The frosting just added to the image.

A deck wraps three sides of the Livingstone home, surrounding the great room and creating a connection between indoors and out.

Daphne Livingstone loves to embellish, and her front porch illustrates this. Even her front door is decorated.

A television was Daphne's concession to modernity in her log home, which is characterized by old-time country charm and a slew of antiques. A loft area adds to the ample allowance of natural light that filters into the great room.

An antique dresser was fashioned into a washstand for the powder room.

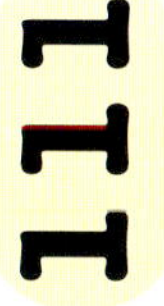

Antiques took on new life in the Livingstone home. In the kitchen, a butcher block island was fashioned from an old treadle machine. An antique scale creates a beautiful suspended display shelf.

The guest bedroom was generously finished in logs, working with the rest of the home's interior, where very little drywall was incorporated.

The loft upstairs creates a perspective on the way the rooflines converge on the gabled roof.

Now in college, the Livingston's son, Tim, left them a legacy in the form of a shrine to his favorite football team.

The master suite snugs into a wing of the first floor, making this a perfect home to grow old in.

Off the Grid

Roger and Kathryn wanted a place where they could escape their stressful lives as attorneys, and they created just that. Their Arizona hideaway, about two and a half hours outside of Las Vegas, is so remote the roads are unmarked and the land around them still serves as free cattle range. They use a special antenna to get cell service at the house, and there are no landlines that reach them. That means no utilities, but they're managing just fine.

Kathryn and Roger Wirth.

This house is powered by solar energy. The entire garage is covered with solar panels. The arrangement works just fine, and this tour illustrates a place where two people find space to simply relax. They do puzzles, read, garden, cook, and just sit back. And they spend a lot of time out on the porch, admiring a view they share with few other human beings.

"It's very comfortable," says Kathryn. "One of our favorite rooms is the garden room. The other favorite spot is our porch. We are actually there about seventy-five percent of our time.

Using their solar panels, they manage to get plenty of water for their garden, where all kinds of flowers add to the scenery, and a healthy crop of tomatoes, chili peppers, herbs, and zucchini adds to their diet. Roger has a very green thumb.

They work on their nest, and they enjoy their environment. "We enjoy hiking a lot and know the area around us pretty well," Kathryn said. If they were to change anything, they might make the garden room a little bigger and porches a little wider. All in all, though, this is their little slice of heaven, just the way they planned it.

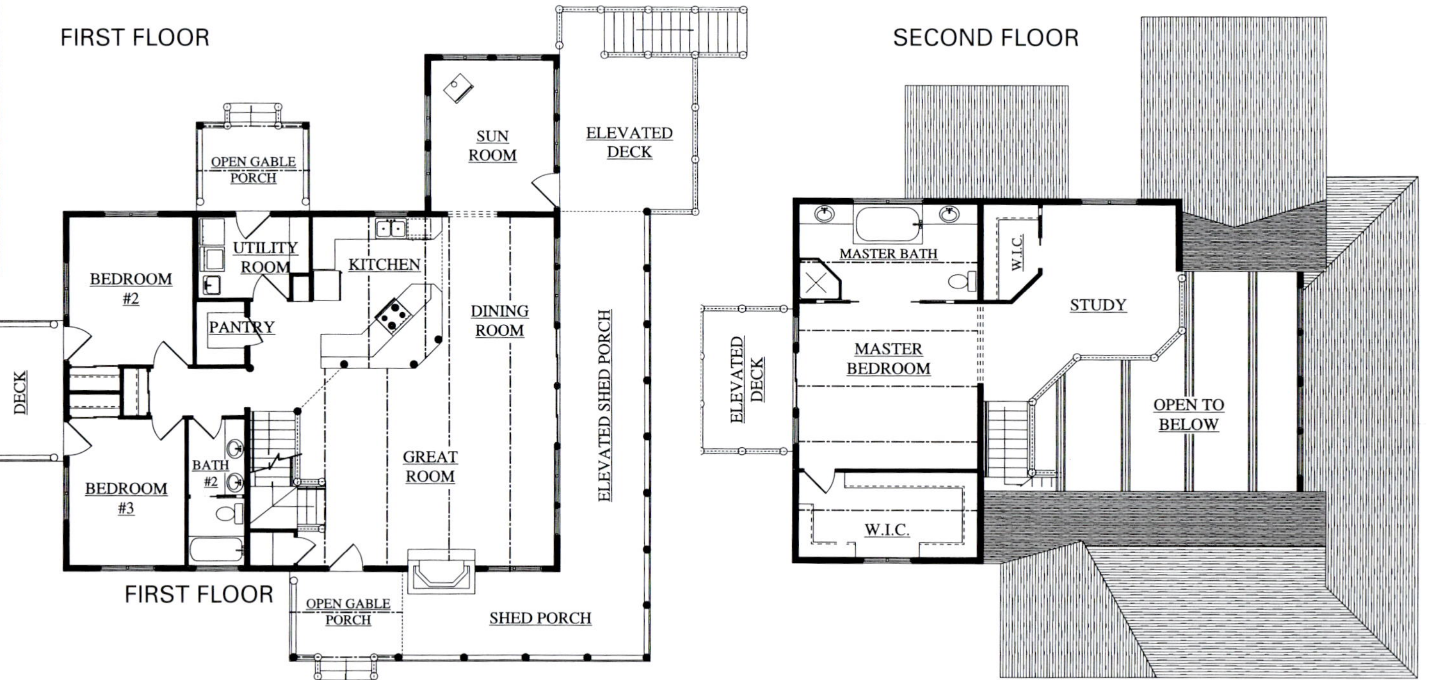

FIRST FLOOR

Set on free cattle range in the open Arizona air, this home is only reachable via unmarked roads.

Incredible privacy is the hallmark of the Wirth retreat, and they find themselves sitting outside on shaded porches during the better part of their waking hours here.

A welcoming entryway highlights the home's log construction. Homeowners chose a square flat log on their home, with round posts and square spindles, stained a different color from the house, which makes them really stand out. "We do a lot of maintenance to preserve the decks and railings, to protect the wood from the sun," Kathryn said.

A sunroom is the Wirth's favorite spot, with a woodstove that chases the chill and provides the primary source of heat for the entire home.

A gas fireplace stands at the ready in the living area, where the contour of the cathedral traces the rise of the staircase. The homeowners collected the stone for the fireplace from around the property.

It's hard to tell that the concrete product Cultured Stone® on the kitchen island isn't the same natural stone as that surrounding the fireplace. The homeowner did the craftsmanship on this project himself, though he didn't do the fireplace because he didn't feel as confident working with the real stone. "Roger is very handy to have around," his wife says.

The homeowners painted the guest room with a faux finish, in a sage color that evokes the desert.

The homeowners used a lot of desert colors for their palette in a celebration of the West. The master bedroom has a half wall to the rest of the house.

Mountain Majesty

"It's more magnificent than we ever expected," enthuses Charles Sangmeister of his new mountain home in Montana. Lana is from Montana, and that played a small role in their relocation after meeting and marrying in the Philadelphia region. Mostly, however, their retirement to Montana was dictated by their choice of home.

"When it came time to leave New Jersey, we were looking at where to go. We wanted a log home, but we knew log homes wouldn't do in Florida, and New England didn't work out for us. Then this land opportunity worked out for us, two years before we left."

The land opportunity was a 275-acre spread. "We wanted twenty acres, but when this land came up, it was something we couldn't resist. Lana has hiked these mountains, and fished this river, and camped here. It's an absolutely beautiful place. When this came up it just fell in our hands, and we said 'Oh God, we've got to take it.' It's great for hikes, it's great to just look at too!"

Lana and Charles Sangmeister.

The dramatic change in lifestyle and scenery has been wholeheartedly welcome. "It has been a great experience to wake up every morning and think, 'Oh My, this is the house we live in.' We walk onto the loft and say, 'My goodness.' And then we look out the windows, and they are absolutely breathtaking. We look out across the Stillwater Valley on one side, and we just can't believe we're here," Charles says. "It's been a great opportunity for us here."

The Sangmeisters lived in a cabin on the property while their new home was being built, and they were fully involved in the process. "We were general contractors and procurement officers, and anything we could do ourselves we did," Lana said.

"Lana knew what the winters were like out here. The log siding and insulation is really what's needed for the Montana winters," Charles said. "We had some idea of what we wanted the house to look like, we knew we wanted it to be log on the outside, and lodge on the inside. But we also liked the idea of having a real openness to it, and also having log and wood accents on the inside."

FIRST FLOOR

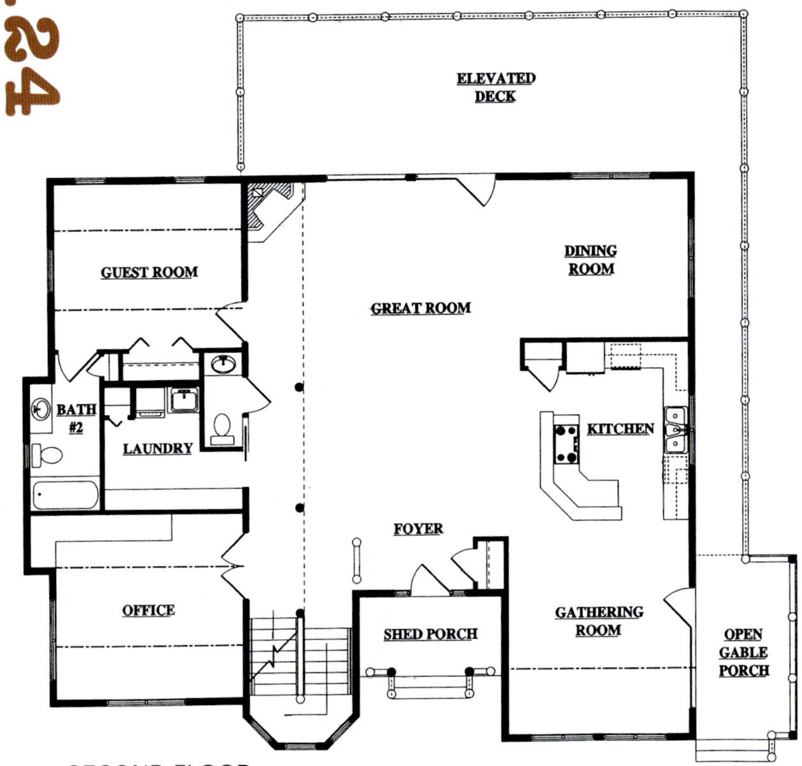

ELEVATED DECK
DINING ROOM
GUEST ROOM
GREAT ROOM
BATH #2
LAUNDRY
KITCHEN
FOYER
OFFICE
SHED PORCH
GATHERING ROOM
OPEN GABLE PORCH

SECOND FLOOR

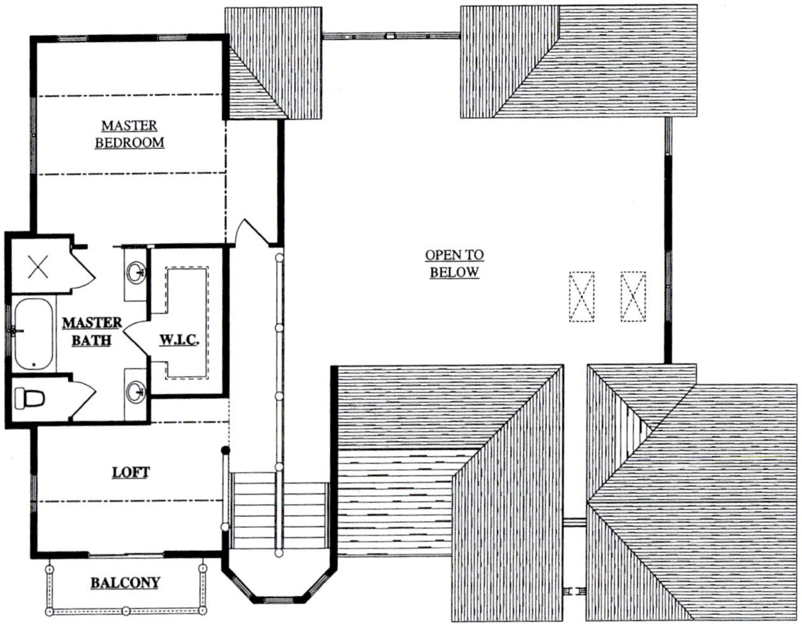

MASTER BEDROOM
OPEN TO BELOW
MASTER BATH
W.I.C.
LOFT
BALCONY

The Sangmeister's nearest neighbor lives half a mile away.

This beautiful home commands incredible views. It's varied roofline, and the silo-like central stone tower, make the home itself part of the beautiful mountain scenery.

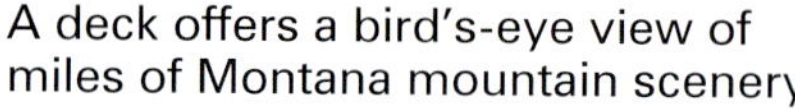

A deck offers a bird's-eye view of miles of Montana mountain scenery.

Lana Sangmeister said she is glad they made their home so open. "We put the kitchen right in the center of the big great room area with the cooktop facing out into the entire house. Charles is a gourmet chef, so it's like he's at the helm of the whole house. When we have guests he can be there cooking and talking to everyone."

"We both end up in the kitchen," Charles said of their new home. "We eat each night at the round table, with candlelight, watching the seasons change. It's a time to wind down."

A dining area on the other side of the kitchen is sized to fit lots of guests. The Sangmeister's love to cook and entertain.

A home office room provides another hangout in this spacious home. "Everyway you look there are windows, so you feel you can reach out and touch the mountains and the evergreen trees," said Charles Sangmeister.

An inviting hearth was tucked beneath the angled roofline, creating a cozy nook overlooked by a balcony.

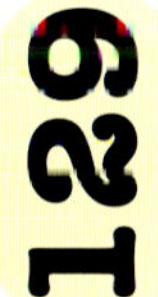

Right at Home

When they had their first log home built, Laurie and Doug Pooch were novices. They had never built a home before. Fifteen years and two grown children later, they set out to do it once again. By this time, they had their own construction company and had a greater appreciation for construction techniques and higher-end materials. With their children grown and gone, Laurie and Doug wanted a ranch-style home. The result is a fair-sized home, with a daylight basement and main living level that surveys a beautiful ten-acre spread. Mature trees grace the yard and provide a welcoming canopy for visitors.

Because their business is now selling and building log homes, special attention was placed on the exterior lighting of the home. "We wanted to showcase and highlight the beauty of the logwork," said Doug. "At night the home looks like a piece of art, and many cars slow down to admire the beauty." Stone with log accents on both the octagonal office and utility room adds drama to the exterior.

"From the minute we moved in it just felt very homey and warm. It just exceeded all our expectations of what we really wanted and hoped it would be," Laurie said. And, as their fellow log homeowners attest, it feels cozy.

Laurie and Doug Pooch.

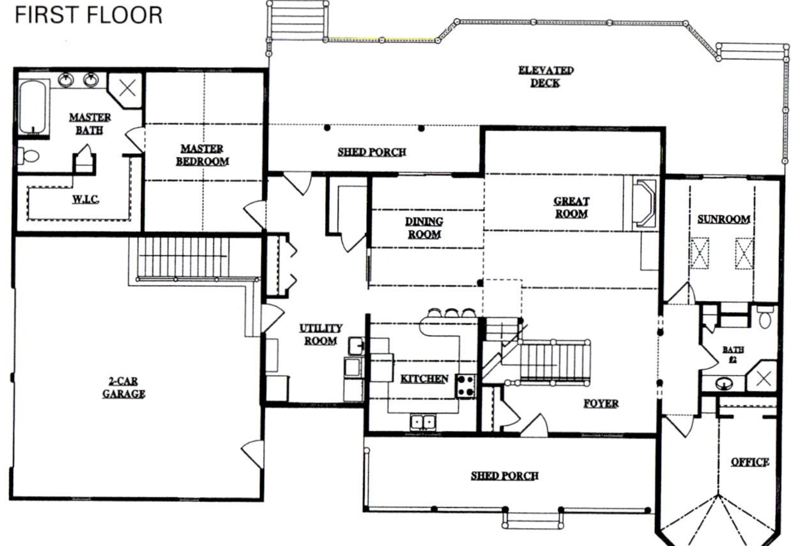

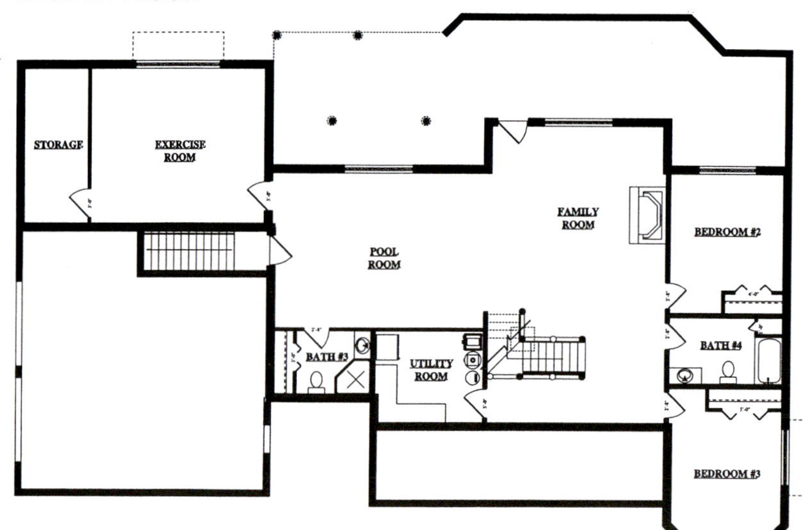

WALK-OUT BASEMENT

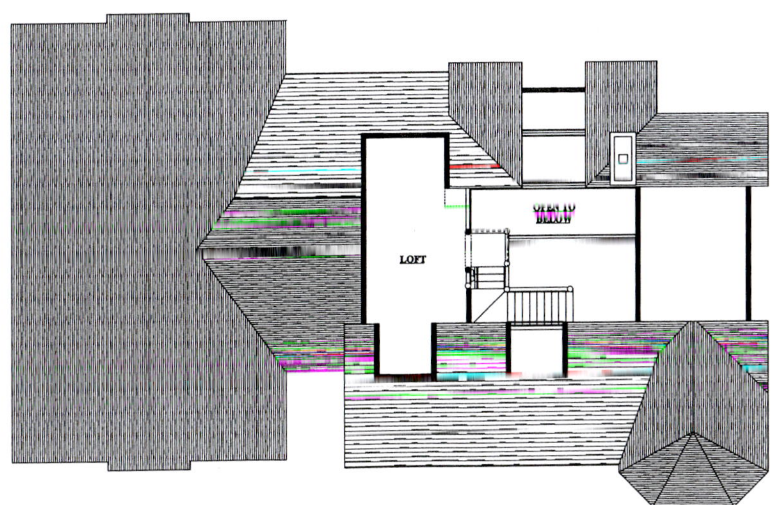

In the back, an elevated deck offers a commanding view. The wide staircase helps create a railing-free viewing area from the windows of the great room, as well as easy access to the landscaped patio area below.

A double garage and two dormers rise up to create interest points on the ridge of this ranch-style home.

A wonderful, shaded front porch allows the owners to look out over the wonderful landscaping created in the center of their circular drive.

A hand-crafted side-table greets guests in the foyer, and offers a close inspection of the peeled logs used to support the staircase.

A stone fireplace and enormous rafters add awe to this great room left and above, illuminated by a wall of windows.

A rock mosaic backsplash creates a centerline in a kitchen rich in wood, from the log rafters and paneled ceiling, to the warm, pine cabinetry.

The sliding French doors in the dining room are framed in half log to match the rafters above.

A corner of the home was dedicated to a home office, accessible from the front foyer. This way, business guests can be welcomed while family life remains separate. A decorative, half log wall with solid log header and supporting log posts in the foyer opens the way to the office on the right, a powder room straight ahead, or a sunroom to the left.

A window seat in the loft area offers a secluded retreat, and a lure for future grandchildren to come visit.

A sunroom is a favorite hangout year-round, with its panoramic view.

The master suite includes a private view of the backyard. The bathroom was finished in painted drywall and tile and has a heated tile floor.

Northwoods Restaurant

In a setting reminiscent of Wisconsin's north woods, this Schereville, Indiana, restaurant features hearty home cooking just like grandma's. The restaurant demonstrates how large logs and open spaces can recreate the feeling of a lodge in a very unlikely location. The building combines Expedition's half-log insulated wall system with big, hand-peeled log posts and accent pieces providing the owners with a log structure that easily meets the different commercial code requirements. Visitors will appreciate the attention to detail in the log work. Bears, eagles, and other carvings were done with a chain saw after the log posts were incorporated into the structure, enhancing the beauty and charm of this log restaurant.

A sign was designed to coordinate with the architecture's log style.

Carved beams present eagle heads overlooking a porch entrance to the Northwoods restaurant in Indiana.

Set on a pond, the restaurant offers patrons a scenic overlook.

Opposite page:
Massive beams overlook the great dining area at Northwoods.

This page:
A lounge area creates a log cabin feel, complete with a mix of comfortable seating.

A gift shop area in the restaurant offers merchandise in keeping with the log home atmosphere.

The bar area of Northwoods.